DISCOVERING DRINGHOUSES

Aspects of a Village History

DISCOVERING DRINGHOUSES

Aspects of a Village History

Elizabeth A Smith

Dorothy Reed

Alan Ramsbottom

DRINGHOUSES LOCAL HISTORY GROUP

First published in 2010 by Dringhouses Local History Group

© Dringhouses Local History Group 2010

ISBN 978-0-9566581-0-4

Produced, printed and bound by:

York Publishing Services Ltd
64 Hallfield Road
Layerthorpe
York
YO31 7ZQ

www.yps-publishing.co.uk

CONTENTS

FOREWORD

A Message from Harry Gration, Honorary President of Dringhouses Local History Group

I have to say that history is, outside of sport, my passion in life. I was a history teacher prior to my life on television. I trained at St John's College in York where my love of the subject was really ignited.

I am fascinated by all aspects of history in York and it is so exciting to be able to focus on the history of Dringhouses, right where I live. The topics that fall under the spotlight in 'Discovering Dringhouses' show how varied local history can be. I am looking forward to seeing the village and its environs with new eyes and I will keep telling my twin boys about Dick Turpin and all aspects of history.

A lot of people have been involved in the preparation of this attractive book and I wish Dringhouses Local History Group every success in their endeavours.

Good luck

Harry

INTRODUCTION

When the Dringhouses Local History Group was set up in April 2005, one of its stated aims was to work with others to promote knowledge, understanding and enjoyment of the history of Dringhouses from the earliest times to the present day. Another was to promote research into the history of Dringhouses and publish the results of such research. In the furtherance of these aims, the Group organises an annual programme of talks, walks and visits, produces leaflets, organises displays, gives talks, and offers help to schools. Now, additionally, we are delighted to be able to publish this book.

Discovering Dringhouses – Aspects of a Village History aims to complement and expand the material previously published locally. The content reflects not only the particular interests and enthusiasms of local researchers who are members of Dringhouses Local History Group, but also the quantity and quality of the documents, photographs, maps, artefacts, buildings and reminiscences.

Dringhouses has more than 2000 years of history and its importance was acknowledged in 1975 when the City of York Council included it in its designated Conservation Area No. 9 (Tadcaster Road). The Area contains the older properties at the heart of the village which was, until the early 20th century, essentially a farming community. Also included are the imposing Victorian villas and their gardens and the area of trees between Tadcaster Road and the Knavesmire. Beyond them towards York, St George's Place, the terrace of town houses on Mount Vale and the Herdsman's Cottage are also within the boundary. With all this, plus an equal amount (including the Knavesmire) outside the Conservation Area, there is so much to explore that the local historian is really spoilt: what to take an interest in first?

Of course, during such a long history, a great deal has been lost. The section entitled *Lost Houses* highlights losses which have occurred in recent decades and we hope that it will encourage greater local awareness and conservation of our significant buildings and a greater sense of place.

Not only is local history important in helping us understand how our predecessors lived, it can also lead down all sorts of byways. It often elicits a "Well, isn't that amazing!" as the detective work unearths yet another unexpected fact or link. We hope the readers of this book will find it enjoyable, informative and not without surprises!

Material previously published locally

There are four books previously published locally. *Halfdan's Heritage: The Story of Dringhouses AD 876 to 1998* by Michael H Pocock (1998); *Hob Moor: Historic Stray and Local Nature Reserve* by Elizabeth Smith, for The Friends of Hob Moor **(2004)**; *The Church of St Edward the Confessor* by Derek Huntington (2005); and *Angles of the Learning Curve: From Mechanics' Institute to York College 1827-2007* by Avril Cheetham, Kaye Green and Marjorie Harrison (2008).

ACKNOWLEDGEMENTS

The Committee of Dringhouses Local History Group gratefully acknowledge all the encouragement and help given by so many people in the preparation and production of this book. The membership of the Group is at the centre of a much wider network of people who have provided invaluable information and support. Those whom we wish to thank include Dr Robert Frost, Yorkshire Archaeological Society, Leeds; Andrew Morrison, Curator of Archaeology, Yorkshire Museum; John Oxley, City of York Archaeologist; Chris Webb, Borthwick Institute for Archives; the staff of the York Archives and Local History Service and of the archives at York Racecourse, and those at the Shropshire Archives, Shrewsbury, the West Yorkshire Archives at Halifax and Wakefield, Northallerton County Record Office, and the archives at Portsmouth and Plymouth; and the staff of York College and Shepherd Group Properties.

Others whom we would like to thank include Catrina Appleby, Michael Bailey, Ray Barker, Les Broxup, A Chapplow, A and B Cocking (Huddersfield), J Cranston, Margaret Elsworth, Jean Fry, Robert Gaskell (Renhold), Marjorie Harrison, Linda Haywood, Allan Henshall (The Regimental Museum, York), Barbara Hickman, David Holland, Mr D Hodgin, Mrs B Lawrie, R and V Little, John Martin, Anne McEndoo, Mrs D Meek, Hugh Murray, Al Oswald, Jim Pearson (Manchester), Mrs C Pidd, David Poole, Marilyn Powell, Derek R Reed, Mrs J Robertson, Mr A Robinson, Dr I Robinson, Mrs R Robinson, George and Daphne Robson, Mrs A Rowntree, Betty and Bill Scorfield, Geoff Shearsmith, Mr B Smith, Richard T Smith (for technical assistance), Dinah Tyszka, Pauline Walker, Edward Waterson and Kay Wheater.

Photographs are individually acknowledged, where the photographer is known. The cover photograph of present-day Dringhouses is by Richard T Smith and the old photograph is from the Les Broxup collection. The part of Samuel Parsons' Map of the Manor of Dringhouses, 1624, on the back cover is reproduced by kind permission of the York Archives and Local History Service.

We would like to thank The Patricia and Donald Shepherd Charitable Trust, The Noel G Terry Charitable Trust, Yorkshire Architectural and York Archaeological Society, and Yorkshire Philosophical Society for grants that they made towards the production costs of the book, and the Sheldon Memorial Trust for providing us with a loan for our project. Without this financial assistance, we would not have been able to publish this book.

Section 9 was written by Alan Ramsbottom, sections 8, 10 and 11 by Dorothy Reed, and the remainder by Elizabeth Smith. All the material has been thoroughly researched, but we would be happy to receive more information and corrections for any factual mistakes we may have inadvertently made.

All possible efforts have been made to trace holders of copyright for material reproduced; we apologise to any whom we may have failed to contact.

A note about reference material used

The authors have made extensive use of census details, civil registers, street trade directories, and material in the York, East, West and North Yorkshire Archives. We have also been able to use unpublished research carried out by Michael Bailey and George and Daphne Robson, and we have referred frequently to the Royal Commission on Historical Monuments of England: The City of York, Volumes I and III, and other standard research texts. A full bibliography for each section has been included in each of the two copies donated to the Reference Section of the York Archives and Local History Service.

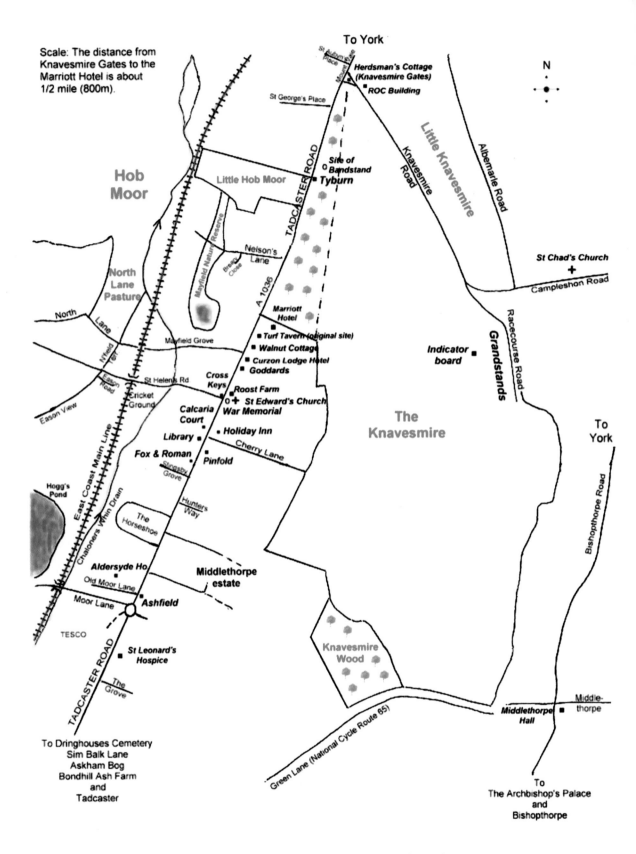

Scale: The distance from Knavesmire Gates to the Marriott Hotel is about 1/2 mile (800m).

To York

N

Hob Moor

Little Hob Moor

St Aubyn's Place
Mount Vale
Herdsman's Cottage (Knavesmire Gates)
ROC Building

St George's Place

Little Knavesmire

Albemarle Road

Mayfield Nature Reserve

TADCASTER ROAD

Site of Bandstand
Tyburn

Knavesmire Road

St Chad's Church

North Lane Pasture

Nelson's Lane
Brecq Close

Campleshon Road

North Lane

A 1036

Marriott Hotel

Wheel Ten

Mayfield Grove

Turf Tavern (original site)
Walnut Cottage
Curzon Lodge Hotel
Goddards

Indicator board

Grandstands

Racecourse Road

Eason Road

St Helens Rd

Cross Keys

Eason View

Cricket Ground

Roost Farm
St Edward's Church
War Memorial

Calcaria Court

The Knavesmire

To York

Library

Holiday Inn

Fox & Roman

Slingsby Grove

Cherry Lane

Pinfold

Bishopthorpe Road

Hogg's Pond

Hunters Way

The Horseshoe

East Coast Main Line

Chaloners Whin Drain

Aldersyde Ho.
Old Moor Lane

Middlethorpe estate

Moor Lane
Ashfield

Knavesmire Wood

TESCO

St Leonard's Hospice

TADCASTER ROAD

The Grove

Middlethorpe Hall

Middle-thorpe

To Dringhouses Cemetery
Sim Balk Lane
Askham Bog
Bondhill Ash Farm
and
Tadcaster

Green Lane (National Cycle Route 65)

To
The Archbishop's Palace
and
Bishopthorpe

Sketch-map of Dringhouses village and environs: features mentioned in the text. (E A Smith)

1.   *TOWN STREET*

Dringhouses, looking towards York, 2010. (M J Ramsbottom)

The most noticeable and the most enduring feature of the village of Dringhouses is the wide, straight main road lined on either side with buildings. The evolution of this important highway can be traced in evidence from prehistoric times through to the present day.

About 10,000 years ago, the retreat northwards of the last ice-sheet left behind a ridge made up of sands and gravels and aligned roughly north-east/south-west in our particular locality. In the millennia before the arrival of the Romans, people seeking to avoid the poorly-drained land on either side used the ridge as part of a much longer east-west trade route.

Three stone axe-heads found in Dringhouses are evidence that people were here in the Neolithic period (5000-2500 BC); they are made of fine-grained volcanic rock from one of several Neolithic axe factories in the Langdale-Scafell area of the Lake District. They have long flat sides, with a sharp edge at the end, and were used in a haft. Polished ones, like those found in Dringhouses, were highly prestigious goods, used as dowry or for trading. Axes from the Lake District have been found all over Europe. We might speculate whether the Dringhouses ones were someone's personal possessions left deliberately or, less probably, whether they were dropped by accident along this prehistoric trading route.

One of the Neolithic axe-heads found in Dringhouses in 1884. It is 11.3cm (4.5") long, of maximum width 5.5cm (2.25"), and 2.4cm (1") thick.

(York Museums Trust (Yorkshire Museum))

It is interesting to ponder at what stage wheeled traffic was first seen along this ancient trackway. An Iron Age wheeled chariot burial has been excavated in recent years at Ferrybridge on the Great North Road and another at Wetwang in the Yorkshire Wolds. Wheeled chariots and carts must surely have been moving along this route during the Iron Age (and probably before), that is, at least 200 years before the Romans arrived.

This already long-established route was subsequently used by the Romans when they built the road linking Calcaria (Tadcaster) and Eboracum (York). It was a short but very important part of their overall network and was included in their Antonine Itinerary, a 3rd-century description of the principal roads of the Roman Empire, giving all the towns along the routes and the distances between them. Sections of this built-to-last metalled surface have been found over the years in Dringhouses. Details about evidence of the Romans in Dringhouses can be found in section 2 of this book.

An archaeological investigation at the Fox public house in 1997 produced twelve sherds (broken pieces) of Iron Age or Romano-British pottery, suggesting settlement immediately pre-dating that of the Romans. This was extremely rare for York as little evidence of prehistoric occupation had been found within the city boundary.

Why a settlement was established at this particular spot is somewhat of a puzzle. However, the reason may perhaps be that this point on the route-way is nearest to a reliable water supply. The stream on the Knavesmire is short and drains a very restricted catchment area, but on the other side of the route the stream, now called Chaloners Whin Drain and flowing alongside what is now Dringhouses cricket field, drains a much bigger area and – more importantly – rises in Askham Bog, an all-season reservoir of water. This drainage pattern has not altered significantly in the last few millennia, so people could well have first settled on the trading route, on the dry ridge, and walked the short distance down to the stream to fetch water. The Romans also would have needed a water supply, but they perhaps sank the first wells: a timber-lined Roman well was excavated in 1973 in the Bishophill area of York. Much later, two wells and two pumps are shown on the 1852 Ordnance Survey map, at the centre of Dringhouses.

Other factors determining the siting of this settlement would include geology: local deposits of sand, clay and gravel would have been very useful. It may even be that a settlement developed in the Ainsty (the area bounded by the Rivers Ouse, Wharfe and Nidd, to the west and south of York) at its boundary with its burgeoning neighbour, the future City of York. There is, however, no evidence of any intersection of routes that would have given rise to the development of a hamlet or village at this location.

Whatever the reason, the village came into being, and in the 12th and 13th centuries the name Dringhouses had several different spellings, 'Dreng' eventually becoming 'Dring' or 'Dryng'. It has been assumed by some authors that the name of the settlement was determined by the 'drengs' living there, drengs being a class of free tenant. However, an alternative and perhaps more likely meaning for the name of the village is 'houses by the drynge', 'drynge' being a paved way. Between Dringhouses and Tadcaster there is a group of cottages called Streethouses, beside the line of the Roman road, here called the Old Street. In parts, the road constructed in Roman times has lasted (albeit buried) into modern times, so when the small settlements were first being established along it, the inhabitants must have been aware of its existence as a route-way, either through encountering the actual surface or through hearsay.

The village of Dringhouses emerges fully from the shadows by the time we reach 1624, the year in which Samuel Parsons drew his map of the Manor of Dringhouses. (This map is considered in detail in section 4.) The main road is clearly defined, wide, with farms and other buildings ranged along it, and the name 'Dringhouses' is written along the road at the centre of the village. The area on the left going out towards 'Sym baulke' is marked in capital letters as 'Streate Landes' and beyond Sym baulke is written 'London Roade'. (A baulke, or balk, is an unploughed piece of land forming a boundary between, and access to, parcels of strips in an open field.)

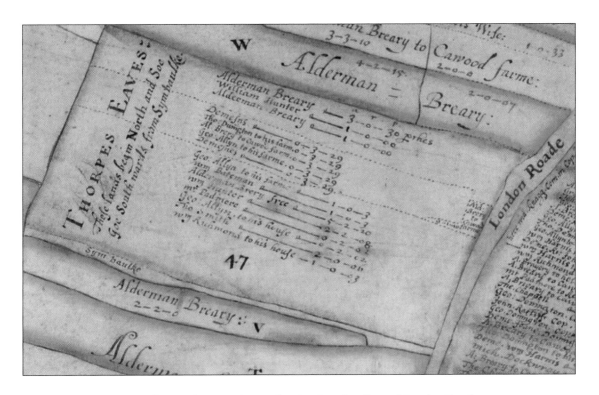

Part of Samuel Parsons' map showing Sym baulke and London Roade.
(York Archives and Local History Service)

Not only do we have Samuel Parsons' wonderful map, we also have excellent information for later decades of the 17th century in a manuscript held by the Yorkshire Archaeological Society in Leeds. It contains several references to Dringhouses as 'the Towne' and to the road within it as 'the Streete', every inhabitant of the village being required to repair his part of it 'unto the midst thereof'. The manuscript contains a wealth of detail about everyday life in Dringhouses at the time and it is the subject of section 5.

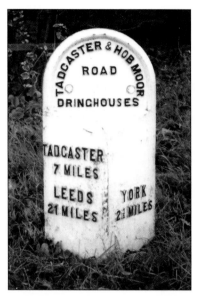

Combined milestones and mounting blocks were erected in 1772 and later replaced with milestones bearing cast iron inscriptions indicating the nearest settlement and distances measured from Ouse Bridge in York. Several are still in place: this one, dating from 1893-4 and used in the Dringhouses Local History Group logo, is near The Grove.

(E A Smith)

The name 'London Roade' recorded by Samuel Parsons on his 1624 map is an early clear indication of the importance of this road passing through Dringhouses. It was the road to the capital, the route by which the sovereign journeyed to York and along which the Sheriffs of York rode out to meet the judges arriving for the Assizes. Dringhouses' villagers must have witnessed many impressive comings and goings! However, measures to ensure the upkeep of such roads nationally became increasingly inadequate and turnpike trusts, able to levy tolls in order to repair and improve roads, were set up. It is no surprise that the hugely prestigious road out of York towards Tadcaster and London was the first of the toll network centred on York to be turnpiked, in 1745. From that year, the Tadcaster and Hob Moor Road Turnpike Trust managed the length of road from Tadcaster Bridge to Hob Moor Lane End (where it met the City of York boundary).

Originally, tolls levied reflected the amount of wear the various coaches and animals were deemed to cause to the road. The charge for a coach drawn by six horses was six times that for a coach drawn by one horse. Waggons and carts were subject to a similar scale of charges; a drove of oxen or cattle was charged five pence per score, and single animals 'not drawing' were charged at one penny. Exemptions were made for traffic to do with legal process and

The turnpike onward to Leeds from Tadcaster. The word 'dial' is perhaps a reference to a sundial on the wall of the toll house at Halton.

(M J Ramsbottom)

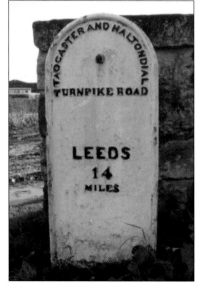

the material needs of local people, for local Sunday worshippers and people going to funerals. Toll booths were set up, the one at Dringhouses being on Tadcaster Road opposite the present Hunters Way. On the 1852 Ordnance Survey map there is a weighing machine marked at this point. It was installed in the early 19th century so that overweight dues could be collected.

Old Toll House, Dringhouses. (DLHG Archive)

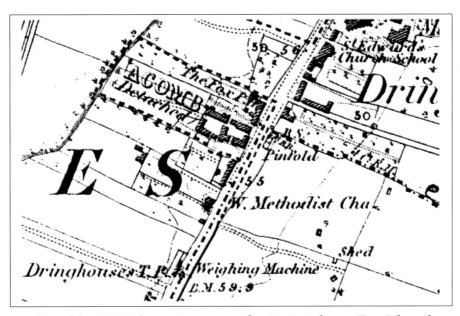

Part of the 1852 Ordnance Survey map, showing Dringhouses Turn Pike and weighing machine at the south end of the village.
(York Archives and Local History Service)

Nationally, income from tolls was significantly affected in the 1840s by the arrival of the railways, and that of the York-Tadcaster turnpike was no exception. Between 1800 and 1840 it had been a well-used route for stage-coaches from York to London, East Anglia, the Midlands, West Yorkshire, and Lancashire. A maximum of around 32 coaches a day passed through Tadcaster in the early

1830s, of which about a quarter were to or from London. With the steep decline in revenue due to competition from the railways, turnpikes gradually became the responsibility of local authorities. The York-Tadcaster road was one of the last ones to be disturnpiked, in 1872. A very detailed and interesting account of this road can be read in 'A History of the Tadcaster-York Turnpike' by W B Taylor in *York Historian* No. 12 (1995).

The Coach and Horses at Tadcaster, photographed in May 2008. Hostelries were found at frequent intervals along the coaching routes and there would be several such establishments in each town. Dringhouses offered the Cross Keys, the Fox (now the Fox and Roman) and the Turf Tavern. (E A Smith)

A journey by stage-coach could be a long, uncomfortable experience! In the 1750s, the York-London service, which ran three times a week, took four days; by 1836 the journey time had been reduced to 21 hours 24 minutes. In a letter written on 24 September 1842 from Boston near Tadcaster to his brother Thomas of Pencraig Court near Ross, Herefordshire, James Brook includes a short description of part of his journey from Ross: *I had an amazing journey from Ross to Gloster* [sic], *excepting being coupled with a little fear; we were no less than 20 outside human Beings & one Dog, Viz 12 behind with the Dog, 7 in front & one on the Top, but soon finding myself too cramped, I stood on my Feet & had a delightful View of the Country, & got inside at Gloster…* It was normal for many more passengers to travel outside than inside the coach, whatever the weather.

The Cross Keys, Dringhouses, in July 2007. There has been an inn on this site since about 1250. The present building, dating from the early 18th century, has had some alterations including, in the late 18th century, the addition of bay windows and the blocking-up of the carriage entrance. The wide archway of the latter can be seen here, with a later porch and door, still the main entrance on Tadcaster Road. (E A Smith)

The 20th century saw great changes in the use of what we now call Tadcaster Road. Trams and then buses and the increasing use of the motor car led, slowly but surely, to the present picture of traffic lights, cycle lanes, bus stops and other 'street furniture'. However, in the middle part of the century, housing development mostly occurred away from the main road so that the old linear village, which dates back at least five hundred years, is still intact. The diverting of the old A64 to a route round the south-east side of York brought alleviation not only to the centre of York but also to Dringhouses. Nevertheless, there are still times when vehicles are brought to a halt by the sheer volume of traffic.

Tadcaster Road in a more leisurely era! (DLHG Archive)

2.   ROMAN DRINGHOUSES

The Romans, in the form of the soldiers of the Ninth Legion, arrived in our area in AD 71. They set up their fortress, called Eboracum, on a spur of higher land at the confluence of the Rivers Ouse and Foss. As we know, the military fortress and the civilian settlement which grew up outside it were hugely important, as is seen in the superabundance of archaeological remains both above and below ground.

The tile tomb found in 1833, reconstructed and photographed in the Yorkshire Museum reserve collection store. This was a cheap form of burial, using roofing tiles from a large building. They bear the maker's stamp: LEG VI SEV, that is, a unit associated with Severus, within the Sixth Legion. About 25 tile tombs have been found in York, but very few elsewhere in England. This one is now on permanent display in the Yorkshire Museum. (York Museums Trust (Yorkshire Museum))

It was the custom of the Romans to bury their dead outside settlements, along the main roads, and in Dringhouses several such burials have been discovered beside the Roman road to Calcaria (Tadcaster). They include a tile tomb (over the body) found in 1833 at Mount Villa, on the corner of Nelson's Lane; a small cemetery found near the St Helen's Road junction in 1903; and a further five coffins found at various sites clustered around the centre of the village. A complete carved tomb-relief of a blacksmith was discovered on the site of the Manor House (where the Holiday Inn is now) in 1860 and given to the Yorkshire Museum by Dr Eason Wilkinson. It is extremely rare to find such a tomb-relief for a metalworker. Such a monument would have been expensive, so this man must have been an important person in the community, or had a rich friend! It is part of the permanent exhibition at the Museum.

A further Roman burial was found during 1997 at the Fox public house site. Previous modern disturbance had removed the skull, the upper rib cage and left arm. On the index finger of the right hand was a copper alloy ring. It was as a result of this find that the name was changed to the Fox and Roman.

The Roman road from Calcaria approached present-day Dringhouses along the same line as our Tadcaster Road as far as Slingsby Grove. Here the modern road continues slightly to the east of the Roman road. A roadside ditch and part of the cobbled surface (the rest remained unexcavated under the pavement and the road) were revealed in 2003 during an archaeological excavation. It was carried out by the York Archaeological Trust at the Starting Gate site, now developed as flats, opposite the Holiday Inn.

This detailed excavation also revealed a burial of an adult female of either late Iron Age or early Roman date, and an infant burial dating from between AD 150 and 200. Intensive use of this area was deduced from evidence of two buildings. One had been truncated by 20th-century activity, so that only traces remained. The other was L-shaped, of large area and with substantial foundations suggesting a two-storey building of some importance. Lack of plaster, mortar and Roman concrete seemed to indicate that the building was made principally

The cobbled surface, part of the Roman road, revealed at the Starting Gate site, 2003. (E A Smith)

of timber, and the presence of many flagons and other evidence encouraged the belief that this could be an example of a *mansio*, a government residence to accommodate travelling officials. It could have been part of a small settlement outside the influence of the military in York itself: other examples of such settlements are known elsewhere in Europe, close to fortresses but not part of them. Evidence of other timber buildings fronting onto the Roman road was also found and a hearth and possible furnace-lining indicated the probable existence of smithing on this site. Nearby, at the Fox and Roman, a dump of metal slag had been found during the dig in 1997. This, together with the tomb-relief of a blacksmith mentioned above, strongly indicates metalworking on a significant scale.

History is acknowledged: Calcaria Court, the new development on the former Starting Gate site. Samian ware is fine Gaulish pottery found on Roman sites in Britain. (R T Smith)

There are several other interesting Roman artefacts found over the years in Dringhouses and now in the Yorkshire Museum, including a handle from an amphora (a huge globular pot for liquids). It is stamped BELSI, the name of a southern Spanish manufacturer, and was found at Goddards in 1980. It is one of only three known to exist, the others having been found at Cirencester and at Avranches (Normandy). A small portable altar for use at home was found in 1934 by Angelo Raine, the then vicar of Dringhouses. An early 3rd-century face vase, of North African origin, was also discovered and would have held a cremation. It is hand-thrown and painted, and finger marks show where the eyes were pushed out and the nose pinched. There is also an unusual single-handed flagon of red ware, with a very narrow neck, found in the 19th century.

The face vase, 19cm (7") high. (York Museums Trust (Yorkshire Museum))

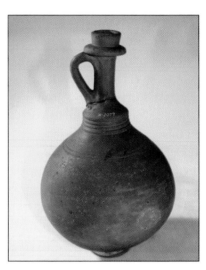

The single-handed flagon, 25cm (10") high. (York Museums Trust (Yorkshire Museum))

Nearby, also in the 19th century, an Apis bull was found on Hob Moor, which at that time included the area we now call Little Hob Moor. It is highly likely that this small figurine, just 6cm (2.25") long, was discovered near to the Roman road; it is a copper alloy model of an animal deity. The cult of the sacred Apis bull, originally practised in Ancient Egypt, became extremely popular throughout the Greek and Roman world. The sacred bull was worshipped as saviour-god of healing, fertility and the future life, and there was a temple to Serapis, an Egyptian god originating in the sacred bull, in the present Toft Green area of York. This figurine is the only one so far found in York and would have been used either as a votive offering in a temple or worshipped at home. It is mentioned here because it was found very near to Dringhouses, and because to have found a link between our area and religious practices of Ancient Egypt is really quite amazing. Like the tomb-relief of the blacksmith and the tile tomb, the figurine is on permanent display in the Yorkshire Museum.

The Apis bull. (York Museums Trust (Yorkshire Museum))

The tomb-relief of a blacksmith, found in Dringhouses. The bearded blacksmith is standing in an arched niche which has a goblet at the top, with a rosette on either side. He is barefoot, with a garment draped over his left shoulder, and is standing beside his anvil, holding a hammer and a pair of tongs. The overall measurements of the tomb-relief are 104cm x 48cm x 16.5cm (3'5" x 1.7" x 6.5"). (York Museums Trust (Yorkshire Museum))

Already a substantial amount of information about Roman Dringhouses has come to light but there must be a lot more to be discovered. Archaeological watching briefs and investigations, both of which are part of the planning process and construction of new developments, reveal more from time to time, as do occasional finds by gardeners! The jigsaw will certainly continue to build up gradually towards a much fuller picture of life in Dringhouses in the Roman period.

3.   THE KNAVESMIRE

For hundreds of years the Knavesmire has been part of the history of Dringhouses. Originally it was the area on which the villagers could graze their animals, but the last hundred years or so have seen a complete change from ancient pasture to what is now an open space for leisure use. Dringhouses people value the Knavesmire as a large greenspace, with views of the Minster and wide cloudscapes.

The Ancient Stray

The flooded Knavesmire, 2 December 2009. (R T Smith)

The Knavesmire, an area of 93.5 hectares (231 acres), is part of the ancient Micklegate Stray, which also includes Hob Moor, Little Hob Moor, Scarcroft allotments and Scarcroft Green; the ownership and management passed from the freemen of York to the City Corporation by Act of Parliament in 1907. The area is flat, poorly drained and subject to flooding, with higher ground to the west (Tadcaster Road), and north and east (Albemarle Road and Bishopthorpe Road). Knavesmire Beck, now mostly culverted, rises near St Aubyn's Place (off Mount Vale), flows the length of the Knavesmire and into the River Ouse between York crematorium and the A64. Various attempts have been made over the centuries to improve the drainage of the Knavesmire by cleaning out the watercourses and by laying pipes. For example, in 1837 Earl de Grey of the Regiment of Yorkshire Hussars gave a large sum towards enclosing the drains. Culverts have collapsed at intervals and have required repair. Most recently, after the abandonment of the prestigious Ebor race meeting in August 2008 due to an unprecedented deluge, a comprehensive drainage scheme was installed under the racing track.

It was precisely because of its natural marshy character that the Knavesmire became established centuries ago as an area for the grazing of animals and not for the growing of crops. (Evidence of medieval cultivation, in the form of ridge and furrow, can be seen on the adjoining slope near the Marriott Hotel.) On Samuel Parsons' map of the Manor of Dringhouses (1624), the area is called Knares Myre, 'Common to Dringhouses, Middlethorpe and Parts of Yorke'. The name probably has the same derivation as Knaresborough (the fortified place or manor house of Cenward) and thus means Cenward's marshy place. Farmers from the three places could put their animals out to graze on it, normally each according to an agreed number, or stint. The Pasture Masters oversaw the welfare of the animals and the maintenance of the common, and by the 19th century their accounts are revealing some interesting payments: for mole-catching; driving cattle to Hob Moor and back for the period of the races; wages and waterboots for the herdsman; and for cutting and piling the main drain. In 1834, income included sums for the grazing of 142 horses and 264 cattle. Right through to the mid 20th century, the custom of the 'breaking of the strays' took place at the beginning of May, when cows and horses were inspected by a vet and then counted as they were led through the gates onto the Knavesmire. By the end of the century, grazing animals were confined to the area of trees by Tadcaster Road, and the historic grazing of the Knavesmire has now ceased completely.

The Herdsman's Cottage

This picturesque dwelling was built in about 1840. It is in the decorative style of 'cottage orné', rare in York. It is of cruciform plan, has one storey plus attics under steep roofs, and stone mullioned bays. The bargeboards are perhaps its most pleasing feature.

The cottage is situated at the northern tip of the Knavesmire, at Knavesmire Gates, the boundary between Micklegate Stray and ancient enclosures to the north (two boundary stones still exist set in the tarmac pavement at the corner of Knavesmire Road and Mount Vale). Some remnants of the old gates can still be seen, and the building, although now surrounded by roads, is very little changed. The 1852 map shows that the cottage had a garden alongside South Prospect Street (now Mount Vale) with a pinfold at the far end. It was here that stray animals were kept until claimed by the owner and a fine paid.

The cottage as it looks today. (R T Smith)

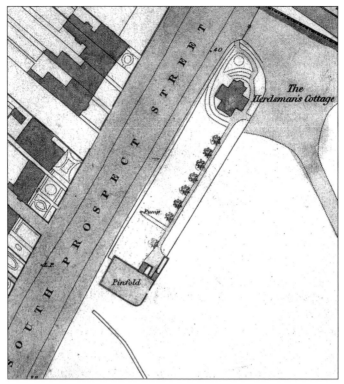

The Herdsman's Cottage as shown on the 1852 Ordnance Survey map (original scale: 5ft to 1 mile).
(York Archives and Local History Service)

Knavesmire Gates in the early 20th century. The access from Mount Vale to the grandstand was put in as a carriageway in 1853 and Knavesmire Road was built in 1921-2. In the early 1900s, the road was still unfenced and cattle roamed freely over the Knavesmire and Little Knavesmire. (York Archives and Local History Service (Maureen Ingram collection))

Racing on the Knavesmire

From 1709, racing in York took place on Clifton and Rawcliffe Ings but, because of the propensity for that area to flood, it was decided to move the races to the Knavesmire. The first races were run here in 1731, the Wardens of Micklegate having been ordered to drain the area and have the ground levelled and rolled. The configuration of the racing track has changed over the years: for example, in 1852 there was an oval course and this was reinstated for the Royal Ascot meeting held in York in 2005. Since then, the bend by Knavesmire Wood has been made less tight by widening the racing track.

In 1755, the first grandstand was built. The architect was John Carr, a stonemason who became the most successful provincial architect of his time, his career being launched by this building. It was one of the most impressive grandstands of the 18th century in England, but in about 1920 it was demolished and partly reconstructed as what is now the Champagne Bar. An external wall can be seen alongside Racecourse Road, the road behind the stands.

The elements which now compose the overall complex of grandstand buildings are, from north to south:

Melrose Stand (1989), so named in honour of Jimmy Melrose (1828-1929), Chairman of
York Race Committee for 50 years.
Stand (c1890): six cast iron columns on stone pedestals; Grade II listed.
Open boxes.
County Stand (c1840): two storeys, eleven bays; Grade II listed.
Ebor Stand (2001).
Knavesmire Stand (1996).
Bustardthorpe Stand (early 1900s).

The grandstands at York racecourse. (R T Smith)

The remnant of John Carr's grandstand. (A Ramsbottom)

The indicator board at York racecourse. (R T Smith)

There is also a small wooden structure with a thatched roof: this is the Steward's Box. Standing in front of the grandstand, and inside the racing track, is the indicator board with clock tower, dating from 1922. Designed by the noted York architect Walter Brierley, it has large swivel panels which were used to show the runners and riders in each race. Although no longer in use, it retains all its original structure and fittings. It is a Grade II listed building and its clock tower is particularly attractive.

York Races have always been popular, apart from during the 1820s and 1830s when the 'nobility and gentry' largely withdrew their support in favour of the meetings at Doncaster. Overall, however, York meetings have always attracted large numbers of pleasure-seekers, with sideshows and cockfights in the 18th century. A detailed account of the characters, both human and equine, who have featured in the history of York races can be read in John Stevens' book entitled *Knavesmire: York's Great Racecourse and its Stories*. One of the stalwarts of racing at York was Col George Wilkinson, Lord of the Manor of Dringhouses. He had a very long association with the racecourse, of which he was Manager, introducing many improvements; he was also Inspector of Racecourses from 1903 to 1933, appointed by the Stewards of the Jockey Club.

Tyburn

The big August race meeting at York was established at that time in the calendar to coincide with the Assizes at York Court and the subsequent punishments carried out at the gallows. Crowds had traditionally gathered to witness this spectacle on the Knavesmire since 1379, and from 1731 could thus walk across to watch the other spectacle of the races…

This place of execution for criminals from York Castle was called 'Tyburn' after the one already in existence near the present-day Marble Arch in London. It was at the city boundary, beside the London road and opposite the access to York Moor, now called Little Hob Moor. The place is now marked by a paved area and a low stone plaque: floral tributes are still laid from time to time in memory of those who died here.

Floral tributes at Tyburn on the Knavesmire. The one accompanied by a detailed explanation was laid at the beginning of November 2007 in memory of 21 Scottish 'rebels' hanged on 1 and 8 November 1746 for their part in the 1745 Jacobite Rebellion. (E A Smith)

Criminals were brought to this spot by sledge or hurdle (a wooden frame) and later by cart, sometimes accompanied along the route from the castle via Castlegate and Micklegate by throngs of people. Thousands would then gather on the Knavesmire to watch the proceedings at the top of the slope. The criminals were hanged from a triangular wooden structure known as the 'three-legged mare', drawn (disembowelled) and, until at least 1795, quartered (their limbs cut off). Sometimes the head also would be cut off and, with the limbs, placed on top of the bars or in other prominent places. Sometimes the body was burnt at the place of execution, sometimes it was sent to be dissected by surgeons, or handed over to friends or relatives for burial.

The Three-legged Mare public house in High Petergate, York. (M J Ramsbottom)

Hundreds of people were executed at the gallows on the Knavesmire. The first was a private, Edward Hewison, aged 20, hanged on 1 March 1379 for rape, and the last was also a private, Edward Hughes, aged 19, hanged for the same crime on 20 August 1801. After this date, hangings took place at the 'New Drop' at York prison: travellers arriving in York from the south had objected to the spectacle. The three-legged mare was, however, not removed until April 1812.

Besides rape, crimes which incurred the death penalty included not only murder, high treason and insurrection, but also housebreaking, highway robbery, forging of wills and money, destroying property by fire (for example, corn stacks; a workshop) and by scuttling (a brig lying in the Humber) and theft, most frequently the stealing of sheep, horses and cattle. Other examples of theft include:

lead and copper (from Scarborough church)
'a great quantity of mercery and linen goods' from a house and shop
breaking open a box and taking out of it 17 guineas (this was merely on suspicion)
the taking of 19 shillings and 6 pence, a lawn handkerchief and a cloak.

Many of those who died were religious martyrs, guilty of no crime against person or property. Sometimes judgments at the Assizes resulted in multiple executions, as on 30 April 1649, when 14 men and 7 women were hanged for various crimes, and on 15 January 1663, when 18 men were executed for an insurrection in Yorkshire. Dick Turpin was, of course, hanged here, in 1739. His legend was created by Harrison Ainsworth in his novel *Rockwood* (1834), but in reality Turpin was a violent criminal, eventually hanged for horse-stealing. He was just one of the many people who died at this place of intense agony, witnessed by huge crowds of spectators.

Changing use of the Knavesmire

The establishing of the racecourse on the Knavesmire in 1731 was, as it turned out, the beginning of a very gradual evolution of use of this open space from pasture to that of leisure or amenity space. Race meetings and executions had long brought large numbers of people to this area but it was the 20th century which saw an increasing variety of use and ultimately the greatest crowds. This development had been foreshadowed by the large attendance which must have been drawn to a review and grand display of fireworks on the Knavesmire on 28 June 1887 for the Jubilee of Queen Victoria.

Between 1890 and 1904, members of York Golf Club had a golf course on an area in the south-west corner of the Knavesmire, near Knavesmire Wood. This seems to be the first example of a ball game being played here and a use of the area which would develop hugely in the following decades. The golfers left the Knavesmire course because of the extreme inconvenience caused to them by horse riders, nursemaids with prams, youngsters stealing golf balls, cows grazing, long grass in the summer, mud in the winter, and greatly increased public use in the summer months. The changing use of the area was already becoming clear.

However, the Knavesmire was used for the grazing of cattle right through to the 1960s. They were removed to Hob Moor for the period of the races and presumably during other large-scale events. The latter included the first Annual Co-op Gala held in 1907 and attended by over 30,000 people; the Great Air Race (Yorkshire versus Lancashire) in 1913; the Yorkshire Agricultural Show (1921); International Sheepdog Trials, for England, Scotland and Wales (1923); and a Grand Military Tattoo (1926). In June 1929, Sir Alan Cobham (1894-1973) flew to York. This famous aviator and pioneer of long-

John Parkin, dairyman, milking cows on the Knavesmire in about 1910, with his daughter. The milk was delivered in churns to shops locally, where it was ladled out into customers' own containers. (DLHG Archive)

distance flight had completed round trips from England to Cape Town in 1925 and to Australia in 1926, and had been the King's Cup winner in 1924. During his visit to York in his De Havilland Giant Moth 12-seater, first the Civic Party and then representatives (pupils and staff) of each of Queen Anne, Mill Mount and Nunthorpe Schools were able to experience a thrilling 10-minute flight from the Knavesmire, piloted by Sir Alan. Later, flights were offered by Aviation Tours (June/July 1931). Other events included Yorkshire Women's Hockey Association tournaments (1950s and 1960s) and the Northern Command Tattoo (1955). The visit of Pope John Paul II attracted a reported 250,000 people in May 1982.

Large events continue to take place on the Knavesmire in the 21st century. Royal Ascot was attended by up to 56,000 people a day in 2005 and the Northern Motor Caravan Show, involving over 2000 caravans, was held here in September 2007. Entertainments include visits by circuses and, in August 2009, a Civil War re-enactment staged by the Sealed Knot. Football continues to be played, hot air balloons take off at intervals, and cycle rallies are held regularly.

The visit of Pope John Paul II, the Knavesmire, May 1982. (R and M Wrightson)

The Bandstand

Mr Spurr's watercolour drawing of the octagonal Knavesmire bandstand. His design included sliding shutters and a flying fox weather vane. (York Archives and Local History Service)

One very popular form of entertainment in the first half of the 20th century was outdoor band concerts. In 1913 no less than 33 performances were given by bands engaged by the City of York's Musical Entertainments Committee during the summer season, on St George's Field, in Clarence Gardens, at Leeman Road Recreation Ground, and in Holgate and on the Knavesmire. A superb bandstand was erected near Tyburn in that year by Messrs F Shepherd and Son, at a cost of £240. It was still there during the 1930s but seems to have disappeared during the Second World War. It was designed by Mr F W Spurr, the City Engineer, and the opening ceremony was a very grand affair, with speeches by Sir Joseph Sykes Rymer, Lord Mayor, and Mr Arnold Rowntree, MP. After the vote of thanks there was a selection of music played by the Band of the East Yorkshire Regiment, which also gave a concert in the evening.

For the opening ceremony there were hanging baskets of flowers, pot plants and shrubs, festoons of fairy lights and Chinese lanterns.

Mr Spurr also put forward, in September 1913, a plan to make the whole of the area between Knavesmire Gates and the present-day Marriott Hotel into a formal park. This area, referred to as 'a strip of waste ground' in 1841, had been added to Micklegate Stray and had become part of the Knavesmire in that year. However, Mr Spurr's grand design, with winding interlinked paths, a pavilion, flower beds, an avenue of trees, shelters, a lake and ornamental ponds, bowling green and aviary, was never implemented. Instead, we now have an area with various species of tree, most of them grown (or still growing) to their full natural height and shape, and including a half-mile-long avenue of mysterious origin. It may have been created in the late 19th century as a promenade or a ride; the ditch alongside may be where material was taken for its construction.

Although adjacent to the busy Tadcaster Road, the whole area offers an environment which feels completely set apart. The trees are beautiful throughout the year. In spring, when the different species come into leaf at different times, the various shades of green are a delight to the eye.

The opening ceremony, 27 June 1913: Arnold Rowntree addresses the crowd. (D Holland collection)

The cover of the programme for the opening ceremony, from the Musical Entertainments Committee Minutes.
(York Archives and Local History Service)

The area of trees, with horses grazing, autumn 1999. (E A Smith)

The Second World War: some reminiscences

Many older residents of Dringhouses and the adjacent areas have vivid memories of the Knavesmire during the Second World War. Racing at York was suspended for the period of the hostilities and the buildings and racecourse were taken over for war use. At first, 'enemy aliens' in transit to prisoner of war camps elsewhere in the UK were housed in the stands. They were followed by about 150 captured German U-boat crews in uniform, whom the local children found to be intimidating and autocratic, walking about in the stands behind a barrier of barbed wire.

Italian prisoners of war then arrived and were housed in huts (similar to those which can be visited at Eden Camp, near Malton) built inside the racing track, near to the indicator board. Football teams from the Railway Institute and the South Bank area used to play matches against the Italians, with no supervising British soldier present. The Italians are remembered as being very friendly towards the locals, with home-made goods being exchanged; they were taken to work on local farms, and some cleared the watercourses on Hob Moor. They left immediately upon the Italian surrender.

The area between the indicator board and Knavesmire Wood was ploughed and food crops grown. The Home Guard manned anti-aircraft batteries of rocket-firing guns beside the prisoner of war huts; on Little Knavesmire club cricket continued to be played on Wednesday evenings. Although the adults were preoccupied with the war, it seems that during this period there was a lot going on to interest the youngsters, especially the boys!

The Royal Observer Corps building

The Observer Corps was an organization set up in 1925 to monitor aircraft movements. During the Second World War (the designation 'Royal' was bestowed on the Corps by King George VI in 1941), the personnel did vital work in protecting the UK against enemy attack. Spotters, trained to identify aircraft, even at great height, by silhouette and/or sound, were stationed at 10-mile intervals throughout the countryside, usually in somewhat primitive accommodation! They relayed their observations by land-line to centres where plotters, seated round a large table, received the messages through their headphones. The plotters then moved counters representing aircraft across the map on the table. Tellers on the first floor gallery overlooking the map could interpret the movement of the counters and could then inform relevant airfields, the police and others so that appropriate action could taken.

After the 'Baedeker' raid on York in April 1942, the York ROC groups were moved from their building behind Robson and Cooper's in Lendal to two new, purpose-built centres, one on the Knavesmire very near to St George's Place and the other on Little Knavesmire, at the Mount Vale end of Knavesmire Road. This latter building is one of less than twenty of this type which were built and, although somewhat altered for its current use as changing rooms, it still retains much of its original structure, including the staircase up to the first floor gallery.

With the advent of the Cold War, the ROC personnel were moved in 1961 to the new purpose-built protected control centre in Acomb; this building is now in the care of English Heritage and open to the public. Although one of the wartime ROC buildings – the one near to Tadcaster Road – was demolished as it was considered to be an eyesore, the other remains. Its role is largely unrecognised but it is nevertheless there as a reminder of the invaluable contribution which many York people made to the war effort.

The Royal Observer Corps building on Little Knavesmire, October 2005. (E A Smith)

As will be appreciated, the Knavesmire has a very long and well-documented history; only snapshots of various aspects have been given above. There is much potential for a more detailed presentation than has been possible here.

4. SAMUEL PARSONS' MAP OF THE MANOR OF DRINGHOUSES, 1624

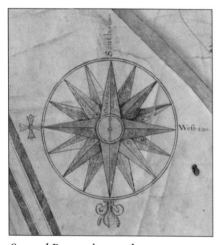

Samuel Parsons' map: the compass rose.

Considering that Samuel Parsons was a surveyor of national repute, remarkably little is known about him or his work. No details of his life are known except that he was working between 1618 and 1639, variously in Middlesex, Essex, Berkshire and Shropshire as well as in Dringhouses. At that time a surveyor was skilful not only in observation, measurement and mathematics, but also in drawing and colouring. In addition, he needed to have a neat, steady hand in order to write all the information in an often very restricted space, as he was using a small quill pen (made from the feather of a crow, blackbird or other small bird). Parsons' map displays all these skills.

The scale, with 'Samuell Parsons me fecit' (Samuell Parsons made me) on the ribbon.

Parsons entitles his map *The Plott of the Mannor of Dringhouses lyinge within the Countie of the Cittie of Yorke.* He further writes: *Taken Anno Domini 1624 and made up 1629 By Samuell Parsons Survaior.*

It is the earliest surviving large-scale plan of any part of York or its surrounding area, and it is amazing that it has survived. It is held by the York Archives and Local History Service, by whose kind permission the whole map and selected extracts are reproduced here. It measures about 97cm by 68cm (38" by 27")

The cartouche giving the title of the map.

and all the writing is perfectly legible. It is a work of art and is highly accurate: if the field boundaries are superimposed on those shown on the 1852 Ordnance Survey map, they coincide in virtually every detail, such was the precision of Parsons' surveying. (Interestingly, on his map of Hubball Mill (1632), which is in the Shropshire Archives at Shrewsbury, his pencil triangulation lines have not been erased.)

In the early 17th century, maps of this type were often commissioned by a landowner in order to have to hand an accurate survey of his estate for management purposes, or when there was a change of ownership of the manor. The whole of the estate was revealed at a glance with, for each property within it, details of its area and the type of tenure by which it was held. Such maps were often accompanied by a written report, but in the case of this map of Dringhouses such a report was either not included or has been lost. At the time of writing, it has not been tracked down.

During the Middle Ages, the whole of the area of the Manor of Dringhouses, except the ings and the commons, was cultivated in strips. We know this because the characteristic pattern of curved ridges and furrows can be seen not only on aerial photographs taken in 1936 but also still surviving in several locations, including the

Medieval ridge and furrow near the Marriott Hotel. This area is called 'The Flatts' on Parsons' map: flatt was a term used in Northern England for a block of strips. Such ridges were created by ploughing in order to create strips of better-drained land, and are most clearly seen when the grass is short. (R T Smith)

Samuel Parsons' map. Probably because of the direction from which Parsons approached Dringhouses (from York), south is at the top of the map. Thus the Manor of Dringhouses is shown bounded by the River Ouse towards the left-hand edge, Bishopthorpe and Coppenthorpe Lordships at the top and Acomb Lordship on the right. The main road out of York is seen clearly, with Knares Myre on its left. Another road nearer the river leads out to Middlethorpe and the Bishop's House.

area by Tadcaster Road adjacent to the Marriott Hotel, in the fields next to Cherry Lane and behind St Leonard's Hospice, in Knavesmire Wood and most notably in North Lane Pasture, part of Hob Moor. This last mentioned, next to North Lane near Northfield Terrace, is the best example of this historical landscape feature in the whole of the Greater York area.

The ridge and furrow behind St Leonard's Hospice. (D Reed)

Parsons' map reveals that in 1624 the cultivation practices in the Manor of Dringhouses were in transition. To the west of the main road, the old system of individual strips being farmed by different people was still in use in the large area of the North Field (accessed by North Lane) and in the very long West Field, between the main road and the stream at the bottom of the slope. Here are written names on each of at least 130 strips, 34 of them being that of A Breary. This system, in which an individual farmer's strips were usually separated by those of several others, was very inefficient although it did oblige the community to work together: sowing and harvesting of crops had to be carried out at the same time by all those farming the strips in one furlong (block) of strips. This system also meant that each farmer had a share of good (and less good!) land.

In the West Field, as in the North Field, after each name the type of ownership of the strip is given, followed by the area of that particular strip. The total area for the West Field is also given: 72 acres, 3 roods and 12 perches. It stretched along the main road almost as far as Bondhill Ash Farm (the modern A64/A1036 junction is superimposed on the field pattern which has been unchanged since this map was drawn); Parsons marks Bondall Close and Bondall Piece at this spot.

To the east of the main road, however, very few individual strips have a name written on them, only those in a field called Thorpe Eaves (just beyond Sym baulke, the ridge left unploughed for access) and several

A small part of the West Field. This map extract also shows Common More Lane, which led from the main road down to a gate giving access to Dringhouses Common (Moore) on the other side of the stream. Common Moor Lane persisted through to the 19th century but is now under The Horseshoe.

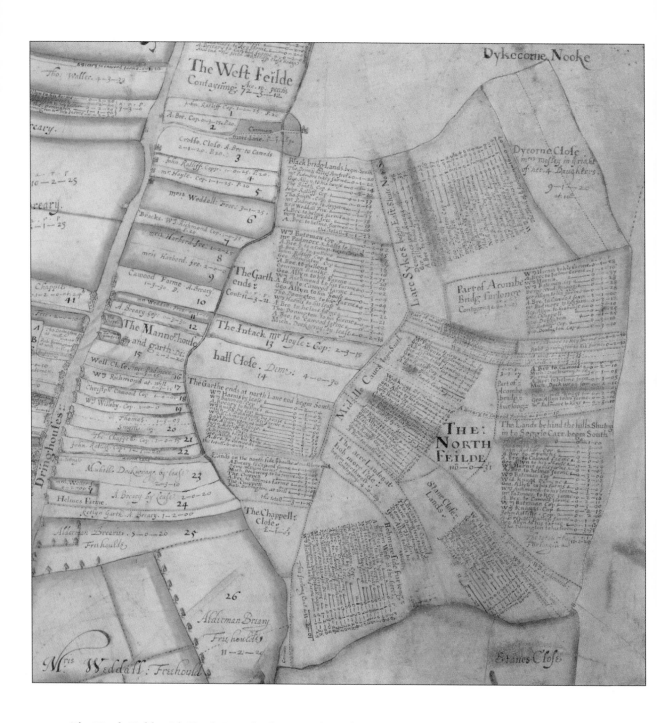

The North Field, with North Lane leading to it from the main road. This shows a typical pattern of strips divided into differently-named furlongs. North Lane starts at the main road just by the letter g of Dringhouses and crosses the stream where North Eastern Terrace is now, at the bottom of the re-named Mayfield Grove. Where the lane turns left, its line is followed now by Northfield Terrace and Eason View.

isolated ones, mostly belonging to Mr Padmore. This gentleman of some standing was apparently choosing not to participate in a new system which had recently been introduced. Owners (but not Mr Padmore!) were exchanging and consolidating their strips, thus creating large parcels of land which individuals then managed as they wished, not in co-operation with others. The map shows that Alderman Breary, William Waller and Thomas Waller, all of whom were significant figures in York, each had a house (in Alderman Breary's case, two) in Middlethorpe, a sub-manor of Dringhouses, and that they had each acquired large areas, much of the rest being designated as Demesne Lands, that is, reserved for the Lord of the Manor's own use. Middlethorpe Common Moor is marked as being 'new enclosed'. The enclosure of common land meant that grazing rights were removed from the villagers and the land was taken over by an individual seeking to increase his land holdings. This process of enclosure and apportioning of the land was eventually completed with the 1822 Dringhouses Enclosure Act.

In addition to the roads and lane already mentioned, the map shows Hobb Lane (leading to Hob Moor) and two un-named lanes leading from Dringhouses to the Knavesmire. One is now called Cherry Lane and the other, just outside the present Marriott Hotel boundary, still existed in 1852 and was called Tyburn Lane. Thus, the pattern recorded by Samuel Parsons has largely survived into modern times.

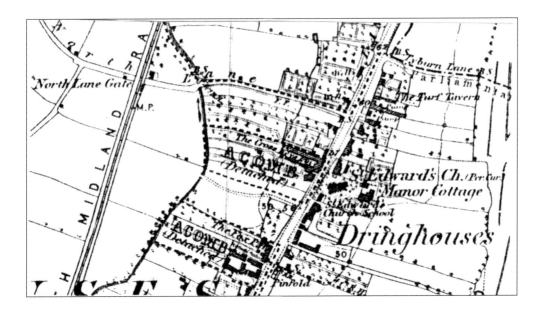

Part of the 1852 Ordnance Survey map (6" to 1 mile), enlarged. In contrast to Samuel Parsons' map, north is at the top of the map. Features shown include Tyburn Lane, the unnamed Cherry Lane, North Lane (which by this stage crosses the railway line at North Lane Gate and continues beyond the old turning to the left) and the curved boundaries of the long plots extending from the main road down to the stream – all just as shown on Samuel Parsons' map. (York Archives and Local History Service)

In the centre of the village, various buildings are named: The Manor House and the Chapel (opposite the end of Cherry Lane); Keyes, Pullens and Helmes farms; George Allyn's house (opposite the end of North Lane), and cottages. The dwellings are drawn very simply and as if viewed at an angle from above, and mostly have two storeys and a chimney. Of different sizes, all except three are shown as being at the road edge and parallel to it – as are the oldest houses in the village today. The larger parcels of land and some individual closes and garths are named. Except for the West and North Fields, the whole manorial estate is contained in a system of numbers (1 to 71) and letters (A to Y), as well as the names of the owners or tenants being included on the map.

The centre of the village.

Thus, Samuel Parsons, in fulfilling his commission to produce a 'plott' of the Manor of Dringhouses, created a detailed, accurate and attractive map, which we are able to admire and study almost 400 years later. Further work could well be done, but meanwhile it is hoped that many people will enjoy this most important record of the village in 1624.

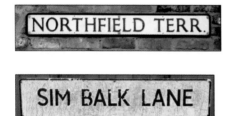

(R T Smith)

5.   BY-LAWS AND FINES

In the archives of the Yorkshire Archaeological Society in Leeds there is a most important manuscript book (reference MD235B(2)/3), of which extracts are reproduced here by kind permission of the Society. It dates from the 17th century and contains details of the 'paines', that is the fines, enforceable within the Manor, imposed on the inhabitants of Dringhouses in 1637, 1638, 1639, 1641, 1643, 1646, 1647 and 1653. These details were set down by the Jury, usually twelve villagers, at the Court held for the Lord of the Manor who, in 1637, was Sir George Whitmore (c1572-1654). He was born in London, the son of a merchant, and became very wealthy; he lived in London, where he was active in politics and held the office of Lord Mayor in 1631-2. He bought estates in various parts of England, including the Manor of Dringhouses which passed to his sons, William and Charles, on his death.

Paines were carried forward from year to year, changing as needed. The Dringhouses document is a contemporary re-writing of several years' paines; in all there are 140 detailed, in 28 pages. A brief statement at the left-hand side of the page is elaborated upon in a short paragraph alongside, and the fine which will be incurred if the by-law is not observed is given at the right-hand edge. Thus we read, for example, that in 1641 no-one must tether horses in the fields where crops are still growing. Anyone who flouts this by-law will be fined three shillings and four pence.

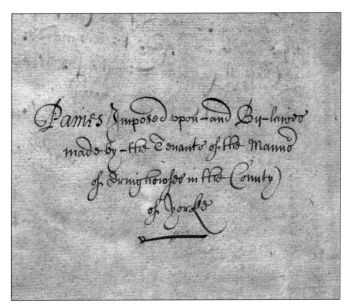

From the title page of the document: 'Paines imposed upon – and By-lawes made by – the Tenants of the Mannor of Dringhouses in the County of Yorke'.

None to take ffire-earke but for the Crowne &c betweene Em-hill and hob-land-end	A Payne laid that noe Jnhabitant shall take vpp any ffire-earth for morter or otherwise, in the Streete betweene Em-hill and hob-land-end except it bee for the Crowne Lyfe vpon payne of eury default	iij⁰ — iiij
eury one to Repaire his part off the Towne Causey to the middst	A Payne laid that eury Jnhabitor shall repaire his part of the Towne Causey vnto the Midst thereof that is against his owne howse or grownd vpon payne of eury default	iij⁰ — iiij
None to Cutt thundlor Wythies	A Payne laid that none shall Cutt or carry away the thundlor Wythies vpon payne of eury burden vijd & one Loade	xs
None to lay dunge but out of theire owne Closes	Item A payne laid that noe Jnhabitor shall carry away any Dunge or Casione out of Closes but their owne vpon payne of eury default	vjd
None to lay hay or within a yard of any Chimnie	A Payne laid that noe Jnhabitor shall lay any Gresse Corne or hay within a yard of his owne or anothers Chimney vpon payne of eury default	iij⁰ — iiij

Part of the Paines manuscript.

32

None to take Fire-earth but for the Towns use betweene Simhill & Hoblane-end	A Paine laid that noe Inhabitant shall take upp any Fire-earth for morter or otherwise, in the Streete betweene Sim-hill and Hob-Lane-end Except it bee for the Townes use upon paine of ev[er]y default	iij^s	iiij^d
every one to Repaire his part of the Towne Causey to the midst	A Paine laid that every Inhabiter shall repaire his part of the Towne Causey unto the Midst thereof that is against his howse Barne or grownd upon paine of ev[er]y default	iij^s	iiij^d
None to Cutt Chandler Whinns	A Paine laid that none shall Cutt or carry away the Chanler Whins upon paine of every Burden xij^d & one Load	x^s	
None to take dunge but out of theire owne Closes	Item A paine laid that noe Inhabiter shall carry away any Dunge or Cassone out of Closes but theire owne upon paine of ev[er]y Default	xij^d	
None to lay Hay et. within a yard of any Chimney	A Paine laid that noe Inhabiter shall lay any Turfes Corne or Hay within a yard of his owne or anothers Chimney upon paine of every Default	iij^s	iiij^d

Transcription of the part of the Paines manuscript reproduced opposite.

From the top of the first page: 'Dringhouses: Paines laid att the Court holden for Sir George Whitmore Knight the seaven and Twentieth day of October in the xiijth yeare of Kinge Charles Raigne 1637'.

During the 17th century, the £ was divided into 20 shillings and each shilling into 12 pennies; the half-penny was also used. The fines imposed were mostly straightforward sums: 12d (12 pence, or one shilling); 10 shillings; and – the most frequently imposed – 3 shillings and 4 pence. This last sum is one sixth of a £ (and also a quarter of a mark, still often used as a unit of currency at the time). Happily, decimalisation in 1971 brought relief from the mathematical challenges of this system!

By far the greatest number (one third of the total) of the paines imposed upon the inhabitants of Dringhouses are to do with maintenance of various features. These include the pinfold, Askham Bridge, Knavesmire Lane (presumably the present-day Cherry Lane), chimneys, hedges and fences, the 'Streete' (the main road), a well, steps and a rail, gates, and especially 'scouring' the watercourses and 'gripping' the lands (making sure they were adequately drained).

The next largest category is 'husbandry', that is, management of the fields – including the crops – and the Knavesmire (used as grazing by inhabitants of Dringhouses, Middlethorpe and part of York), and animals. Ten paines set out exactly how many turfs can be taken and by whom – turfs were cut pieces of peat, the size of bricks, used as fuel. A further ten paines detail the fine payable for the unlawful cutting of hedges, whins (gorse) and quickwood (hawthorn).

Fire must have been an ever-present threat as it is forbidden to put hay within a yard (1 metre) of a chimney or oven, to thresh by candlelight and to carry fire between houses. No-one is to take fire-earth (clay) except for the village's use, and several times there is mention of not taking in vagrants 'or other wandering persons', also referred to as 'rogues or beggers', and the villagers are not to steal dung (the only fertilizer available) from others. In the later paines – those of 1648 and 1653 – loads of stones are to be brought, presumably because the access lanes to the fields and to the Knavesmire were in such a bad state. (In 2008, stones were brought to Hob Moor as the area near the North Lane/Chase Side Court access was in an extremely muddy condition.)

It is difficult to appreciate what the deterrent effect of the fines may have been. There is a significant spread of amounts payable, from 3d to 39/11d. This latter sum is almost £2 (and thus 160 times greater than the smallest fine imposed), and the highest fines will be imposed in very few circumstances. Villagers must take in only 'able' tenants; take only the usual way to get to North Field (people must have been taking short-cuts across the strips under cultivation); Mr Driffield is to take no more than one tenant; George Allen and Thomas Donnington are to make up (reinstate) their fences; and Mr Fairweather is to avoid Edward Knowles! Each of these heavy fines perhaps reflects what had become a persistent misdemeanour which needed to be dealt with by strong measures and the fines will be imposed if these by-laws are contravened.

The Jury members are named in 1639, 1641 and 1643, and some of these men are also named in one or more of the paines laid. George Allen seems to have been one of those least willing to observe the by-laws, five of which are made specifically for him. For example, in 1647 he was required to 'make up' (make good) one of his fences and the fine for non-compliance was three shillings, a considerable sum. After the paines section of the manuscript, details are given of 'presentments' (statements made on oath) made by the Jury at the Court held for William Whitmore and Charles

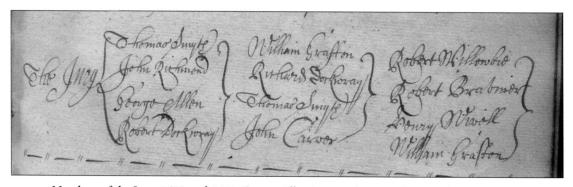

Members of the Jury, 1659 and 1661: George Allen is named, as are the two Thomas Smyths.

Whitmore on 6 April 1659. There are 18 such statements of complaint against villagers and George Allen is named in no less than seven of them. His misdemeanours include leaving one of his fences down; tethering two mares and foals in the cornfield; not serving ale at the statutory price; neglecting his office of by-law man (whose role was to enforce the paines!); and failing to scour his watercourses. This man was obviously a force to be reckoned with in the village at that time!

Thomas Smyth junior is also mentioned in the presentments for not selling ale at the correct price. On his map of 1624, Samuel Parsons wrote the name 'Thomas Smyth' on the plot where the Cross Keys inn is now. Presumably the Thomas Smyth of 1624 was the father of the Thomas Smyth junior named in the presentments in 1659.

As in the case of Samuel Parsons' map, we are really privileged to have such important information about the village of Dringhouses in this paines manuscript. It gives us an invaluable insight into the lives of the villagers during the middle of the 17th century and is so detailed that it could well be the subject of further study.

Two of the oldest buildings in Dringhouses still have features dating back to the 17th century. No 23 Tadcaster Road, now the Curzon Lodge Hotel (formerly called The Beeches), was built in the 17th century, if not earlier. It comprised three rooms; between two of them is an original chimney-breast, over 3m (9 feet) wide, hidden by Georgian alterations. Likewise, the whole house was encased in brick in the 18th century, so no part of the original is visible externally.

However, Walnut Cottage, formerly three separate dwellings, still has observable features dating back to the 17th century. The oldest part is the section nearest to the Marriott Hotel and it originally consisted of a low cottage of one storey and attics. It was given a new front and an upper storey in the late 18th century but in the north gable the original old part can be seen in the tumbled brickwork, which shows the original roofline, together with blocked two-light windows. The steep pitch of the roof of Walnut Cottage reveals that it was once thatched (as most of the houses in Dringhouses must have been), the steep pitch facilitating rapid run-off of rain.

Walnut Cottage, originally three separate dwellings.
(E A Smith)

The heightened north gable of Walnut Cottage, showing the tumbled brickwork of the 17th-century roofline. (E A Smith)

6.   KNAVESMIRE WOOD

Knavesmire Wood is an area of 5.6 hectares (13.8 acres) of mature broad-leaved woodland just outside the south-west corner of the boundary of the Knavesmire. It has significant value for wildlife, and forms a prominent landscape feature for walkers, joggers and cyclists who frequent the area and for racegoers, not to mention all those who watch York races on television: a section of the racing track runs alongside the eastern boundary of the wood.

The southern end of Knavesmire Wood, with the old Green Lane now surfaced and part of National Cycle Network Route 65 (York to Selby section). (M J Ramsbottom)

The early history of the wood is far from clear; research has not yet revealed who was responsible for its creation. However, some conclusions can be drawn from map and other evidence. Samuel Parsons' very accurate and detailed map of the Manor of Dringhouses (1624) shows that there was no wood at that date. An etching by William Lindley entitled 'A View of the Grand Stand and part of the Horse Course on Knavesmire near York' and dated c1760 shows a good number of trees at the southern end of the Knavesmire and elsewhere, although these could have been included by the artist for aesthetic reasons.

In 1772, John Lund junior drew four somewhat basic maps, one of each of the four York Wards and Strays. That of Micklegate Ward has lines of trees in a small area just outside the southern boundary of the Knavesmire and, given the inaccuracy of the boundary-line drawn by Lund, this must be a representation of Knavesmire Wood. The same tree symbol is used by Lund in only one other instance: to show the trees along New Walk. In 1731, 1732 and 1740, a total of 460 limes and elms were planted along the riverside walk, at first from the city walls alongside St George's Field and later for a further ¾ mile beyond the Foss. An etching and engraving by Charles Grignion after Nathan Drake entitled 'Prospect of a Noble Terras Walk' (1756) shows mature trees along New Walk and it is possible to conjecture that the Knavesmire trees and those along New Walk were planted at roughly the same time and at least in part for the same reason: to enhance the landscape. The Manor of Dringhouses was purchased by Francis Barlow of Middlethorpe Hall in 1718 and he may well have created the wood, which is visible from the Hall.

Jefferys' map of Yorkshire (1771), held at the Northallerton County Record Office, does not show Knavesmire Wood, but this area of the map shows very few trees and only those near habitations; the principal features marked are roads, lanes, named settlements and individual buildings (houses and chapels). It can reasonably be concluded that Knavesmire Wood was in existence at the time but was not recorded by Jefferys, as it is not possible for it to have sprung into being as a landscape feature between 1771 and 1772, the date of John Lund's map.

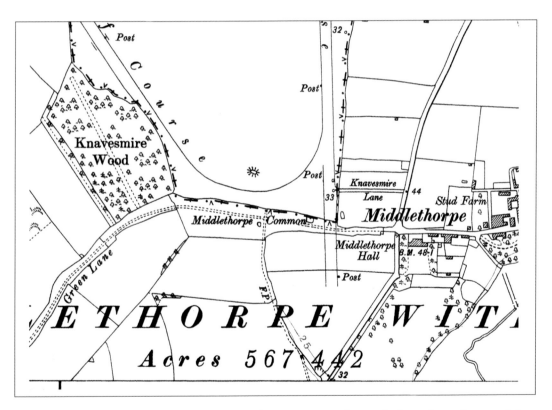

Part of the 6" Ordnance Survey map surveyed 1846-51, revised 1907. It shows Green Lane and the relationship between the wood and Middlethorpe.

Be all this as it may, the wood with its central avenue is clearly shown on Francis White's plan of the City of York and the Ainsty (1785) and, now named Knavesmire Wood, on Robert Cooper's map of the Ainsty (1832). This latter map shows very clearly that the only access to the main avenue, and to the wood as a whole, is from the green lane linking Sim Balk Lane to Middlethorpe Hall and the hamlet of Middlethorpe. The avenue ends abruptly at the northern end (where there was a stream) and is not continued by any path. This configuration is shown also on the 1852 6" Ordnance Survey map and on others through to the 20th century.

The present-day wood has several interesting features. It has a dry stream boundary on the north-east side and a ditch boundary on the southern edge. In the north-eastern part, medieval ridge and furrow can still be clearly seen, aligned NNW-SSE, and the central lime avenue, 320 metres (350 yards) long, is on a ridge on the same alignment.

The main avenue. (M J Ramsbottom)

The avenue may have been developed as a vista through the pre-existing wood, its orientation being determined by that of the ridge, or it may have been planted as a significant landscape feature and beautiful walk, with the wood developing subsequently. Such avenues were indeed created as walks in the 18th century and there was already an example, planted in the early 1700s, in the grounds of the Archbishop's Palace at Bishopthorpe. (Sadly, this avenue was felled, probably during the 1960s.) Francis Barlow, whose father was from a West Riding middle-class background and built Middlethorpe Hall in 1702, inherited the property in 1713 and in 1718 bought the Manor of Dringhouses. Planting a long lime avenue could well have been due to a wish on his part to establish himself more securely as a member of the gentry. The grounds of the Hall were too small, constricted as they were by the hamlet of Middlethorpe, the road to Bishopthorpe, and watercourses. The site of the lime avenue was probably the nearest available suitable location which, moreover, from 1731 (when York races moved from Clifton Ings to the Knavesmire) was visible to all those who attended the race meetings.

The lime avenue is the most distinctive feature of the whole wood. Some of its oldest trees have had to be replaced, and other management of the crowns has been carried out. Present-day aerial photographs (for example, that of the Photomap of York, 1999) no longer show the distinctive line of lime tree canopies which is visible on those taken in 1936, 1967 and 1972. William Hargrove wrote in 1818 of the walk in the Palace grounds 'extending between a double row of lofty and luxuriant lime trees, the branches of which, by uniting above, form a lengthy canopy … highly admired

The base of one of the old limes, spring 2009.
(M J Ramsbottom)

Aerial photograph, 1936 (copyright, Blom Aerofilms). This shows that each line of trees is composed of about 40 canopies. Photographs taken after 1966 show the number to be reduced by almost half. More recently, it was noted that 22 old limes and seven old lime tree stumps remained.

by every observer'. The same doubtless applied to the Knavesmire Wood avenue, as it must surely have been created to be admired. Even today it is very impressive, with the older trees exhibiting their typical growth of twiggy sprouts around the bole and exceptionally strong buttressing at the base.

Other trees of note include, at the south end of the wood, two very old beech and a line of old hornbeam. At the south end of the main avenue is an oak tree which may well be over 400 years old.

The greater part (4.81 hectares) of Knavesmire Wood was owned by York Corporation which in 1965-6 removed decayed timber and planted new lime saplings as eventual replacements for the older trees. The Woodland Trust acquired this acreage in 1990 as a gift from York City Council and has carried out further management work. The woodland is well-structured, with different heights and ages of trees and a good variety of species in spite of the dominance of sycamore. The high canopy, combined with a variety of understorey, results in favourable conditions for many birds and animals; there is also a rich ground flora.

An exchange of letters in 1941-2 between York Corporation and the Commandant of the prisoner of war transit camp on the Knavesmire reveals that soldiers were taking timber from Knavesmire Wood. This probably accounts for much of the sycamore regeneration apparently being about 50-60 years old. However, this cannot have been the only instance of the wood being plundered!

Local people remember the wood as it was in the 1960s and 1970s with ditches on all sides except the west, and a timber fence which failed to keep children out. The scouts from St Chad's Church, Campleshon Road, used to range over this area as part of their 'wide' (ie far and wide) games and had band practices (with loud bugles!) in the wood. Tales were told of 'Watercress Charlie', a tramp who was rarely seen but whose existence scared the local children. Some people used to collect leaf-mould for their gardens. At this time, the wood is remembered as being denser than it is today, with more undergrowth. Many people have fond childhood memories of being able to play unsupervised there. The most spectacular event within living memory was undoubtedly the demolition of a small York Corporation sewage works at the western edge of the wood: it was blown up as an exercise by the Territorial Army in the 1950s. Some remnants of the structure can still be seen.

Drifts of wood anemone in Knavesmire Wood, April 2009.
(Iris Wells)

Nowadays, Knavesmire Wood is under considerable pressure as a local amenity, being a popular place to walk, with or without dogs, but it has high landscape and conservation value. It is a magical place, especially on still, frosty days. Even on the hottest days of summer it offers a cool haven. Perhaps it is at its most delightful in early spring, when the trees come into bright-green leaf; wood anemone and wood-sorrel flower in drifts before the canopy closes, and the wood is filled with birdsong.

About the Common Lime and Lime Avenues

The common lime is found abundantly in towns and in the countryside; it is the tallest broad-leaved tree in most areas and in Britain as a whole. Its original name was the Linden Tree but in Britain in the early 17th century it acquired its alternative name of Lime.

Limes were extensively used in the second half of the 17th century to create formal walks and avenues which however declined in popularity in the later 1700s. Doubtless the common lime was chosen for its impressive height (usually up to about 40 metres), its exuberantly large crown and its fragrant flowers. During the 20th century it was extensively planted along streets. Unhappy motorists continue to bewail the sticky secretions which fall onto parked cars from the aphids feeding on the greenery above!

Nationally, impressive lime avenues are few and far between, being most usually found in the grander landscapes of very large properties. The lime avenue in Clumber Park, near Worksop, is the longest of its kind in Europe; it was planted in 1840 and is two miles long. The nearest long avenue to Dringhouses is at Castle Howard, where the road to the north of the obelisk passes between rows of massive lime trees planted in 1709. The short lime avenue in front of Beningbrough Hall is the third in the history of the property, the original one having been planted in the 1700s (the Hall itself dates from 1716). That original one was replaced in the late 19th century and the two old limes at the end of the present avenue are most probably survivors of that second planting. The most recent replacement avenue was planted in the mid-1990s. It may well be that the Knavesmire Wood lime avenue was also replaced at intervals throughout its history; the two old limes at Beningbrough and the oldest Knavesmire Wood ones could well be of similar age, their difference in height and girth being due to their different growing conditions.

The traditional material of English wood carvers was oak but the renowned Grinling Gibbons (1648-1721) is remembered particularly for his spectacular high-relief carving, especially of flowers and foliage, in limewood. He was born in Holland and arrived in England c1667, where he worked first in York, under architect and builder John Etty (c1634-1708). He then moved to London: the splendid lime and oak carving in the Choir of St Paul's Cathedral is his work. Later, he worked also in marble and stone, and the full-length figure of Archbishop Richard Sterne (died 1684) in the North Choir Aisle of York Minster is by him. There is a portrait of Grinling Gibbons (on loan from the National Portrait Gallery) in Beningbrough Hall, on the first floor landing. Coincidentally, Simon Jenkins, in his book *England's Thousand Best Houses*, considers that the drawing room at Beningbrough Hall 'has carving worthy of Grinling Gibbons'. This is a reference to the splendid example of limewood carving, originally painted, over the two doors.

Lime flowers, Knavesmire Wood, June 2009. (E A Smith)

The lime avenue in Knavesmire Wood is a very special feature, to be much valued, appreciated and respected.

Looking towards Middlethorpe Hall from Knavesmire Wood. (E A Smith)

7.   *THE SWANN AND DIXON FAMILIES*

George Swann (1799-1868) and John Swann (1793-1872) were both bankers, partners in the much-respected York firm of Swann, Clough and Co. The bank's first title (in 1771) was Willoughby, Raper, Clough and Swann, and it continued in existence until 1879 when, due principally to former partners having had sizeable overdrafts, it failed. George and John were cousins and were grandchildren of Thomas Swann, butterfactor, of Micklegate. Not only were they closely related and rich; their wives were sisters, from Liverpool.

George Swann of Ashfield

George Swann's very early existence is mentioned in two letters in the correspondence of the Lister family of Shibden Hall, Halifax. In a letter from York dated 19 April 1799, we read : *Mrs Swann is in an increasing way.* Mrs Swann was thus expecting George at this time. In the other letter, also from York, dated 28 November 1901, later news is given. *Mrs Swann is tolerably well, but she looks so delicate at times one would suppose a Blast of Wind wd* [sic] *blow her over. George has been very ill with cutting his teeth.* This correspondence, which includes these early references to George and his family, shows us that already the Swann family was moving in the circles of the gentry.

George married Frances Elizabeth Dixon in the parish church of Renhold, Bedfordshire, on 11 April 1835. One of the witnesses was Edward, a brother of Frances, and the other was Fanny M Polhill, presumably a friend of Frances and a member of the only monied family in the area of Renhold at the time, the Polhills of Howbury Hall. For the time being, it remains a mystery how this connection with Renhold was made and why George and Frances chose to marry so far from home.

By 1838, George and Frances had bought a property just south of Dringhouses; it was called Ash Tree Farm and it was here that they brought up their family. A plan drawn in 1842 shows a large house with yards and offices, an extensive garden and ornamental grounds, and an ice-house. The fields belonging to the farm are shown extending as far as Sim Balk Lane to the south and to the stream along the eastern boundary.

By the mid 19th century, most large country houses had an ice-house in the garden. Ice, either imported or gathered locally during the winter months, was stored in the ice-house which usually consisted of an ice chamber, partly underground, insulated by the use of straw in the cavity between its brick walls. The chamber was approached through an entrance passage with access doors, and there was a drain, also known as a sewer. The structure was usually domed and covered with soil and turf. The ice would have had culinary uses (for preserving fish, meat and dairy produce and in the preparation of desserts), as well as being used to cool wine and for the treatment of fevers.

The name of Ashtree Farm was changed at an early stage to Ashfield and a brochure from 1873, when it was sold by auction, shows the residence very much as it survived through to the 21st century. A plan of the ground floor is given and the property is said to be 'very valuable and attractive', comprising 83 acres of first-class land and an excellent family residence, of modern construction, containing 4 reception rooms and 13 bedrooms, with well-arranged outbuildings and servants' offices. Detached are a bailiff's house,

The ice-house near Monk Bar, York. It is just outside the city wall, behind the Keystones public house. (E A Smith)

with complete farm buildings, and yard, stables and coach-house. Other details given demonstrate that the property 'offers unusual facilities to a hunting man'. Such was the family home of George and Frances Swann.

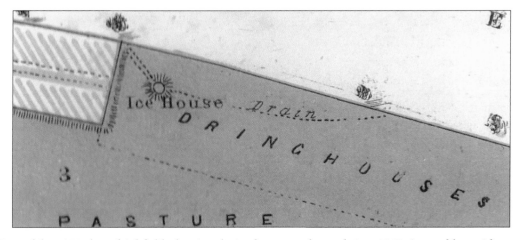

Part of the 1873 plan of Ashfield, showing the ice-house, unchanged since 1842. Some older residents of Dringhouses remember this structure, with its tunnel, as it was still there in the 1940s.

(York Archives and Local History Service)

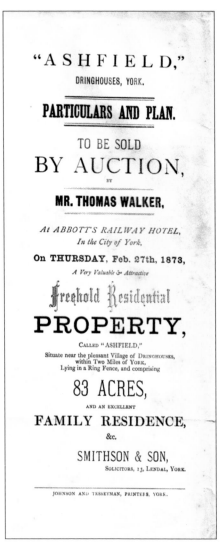

"ASHFIELD,"

DRINGHOUSES, YORK.

PARTICULARS AND PLAN.

TO BE SOLD

BY AUCTION,

BY

MR. THOMAS WALKER,

At *ABBOTT'S RAILWAY HOTEL,*
In the City of York,

On THURSDAY, Feb. 27th, 1873,

A Very Valuable & Attractive

Freehold Residential

PROPERTY,

CALLED "ASHFIELD,"

Situate near the pleasant Village of DRINGHOUSES,
within Two Miles of YORK,
Lying in a Ring Fence, and comprising

83 ACRES,

AND AN EXCELLENT

FAMILY RESIDENCE,

&c.

SMITHSON & SON,

SOLICITORS, 13, LENDAL, YORK.

JOHNSON AND TESSEYMAN, PRINTERS, YORK.

Ashfield: the front of the 1873 sale document. (York Archives and Local History Service)

The gravestone of George and Frances Swann in York Cemetery. As early as 1843, George had bought two plots, one of which remained unused, in the centre circle (the most prestigious area). (R T Smith)

The Swann family must have lived very comfortably at Ashfield: the 1861 census records the parents and four surviving children, a butler, footman, housekeeper and housemaid. George died on 2 March 1868 and the *Yorkshire Gazette* of 14 March carried an account of his funeral, with details of the coffin and mention of the crest of the deceased.

The procession from Ashfield to York Cemetery comprised about six mourning coaches and several private coaches. Swann family members included the three Misses Swann (George's daughters) and T Swann (his son), but not his widow; however, two of Frances' brothers attended. Several traders in the centre of York closed their shops as a mark of respect. George was buried in a vault where the remains of his widow were also interred later. Having sold Ashfield in 1873, Frances was living at 13 Mount Vale at the time of her death on 19 October 1884.

Is this the Swann crest, a head set within swan feathers? This hopper-head was on the rear wall of Ashfield in August 2007. (M J Ramsbottom)

The Swann children

Two of the Swann daughters married well; moreover, they did so noticeably soon after their father's death in March 1868. In 1869, the eldest, Fanny Annabella (born in 1837), married Vincent Charles Stuart Wortley Corbett, a mining engineer, and lived for most of the rest of her life at Houghton-le-Spring, on the Durham coalfield, where her husband had a very long and distinguished career. Nearby, there was an Annabella pit – the name is surely not a coincidence. In 1870, the second daughter, Georgiana Elizabeth, married William Cary, a gentleman farmer, who became a land agent; they spent many years in the Milnthorpe area (south of Kendal), where he was managing large estates. Their sister, Emily Mary, the third of the Misses Swann who were so regularly involved in the life of the village of Dringhouses, including its church and school, never married. Their brother, Thomas William, became a banker initially, but the *Yorkshire Gazette* carried news of the death, on 6 July 1896, at Falmouth, of the Rev Thomas W Swann, only son of George Swann, deceased, of Ashfield, York.

Ashfield: the front of the property in 2007. (J Maskill)

The Dixons of Liverpool

The 1851 census for Ashfield reveals that Edward Dixon was visiting his sister, Frances Swann, and her family there. Edward and Frances were two of eight children born to Henry Dixon and Catharina Townley Plumbe. All the children were born and baptized in Liverpool, where the family lived at Brook Farm, but there were already strong connections with Yorkshire. Henry came from the notable Dixon family of Gledhow, Leeds, and Catharina's family was not only of Wavertree Hall, Liverpool, but also of Tong Hall, Bradford, and the marriage took place at Tong church on 28 April 1794. This pre-existing link with West Yorkshire is probably part of the reason why so many members of this family eventually resided, and in some cases were buried, in York or Yorkshire. Catharina died at Brook Farm in 1819 and Henry Dixon (1766-1844) lived for the last years of his life in South Parade, York, with his unmarried sister, Mary. Mary, Henry and one of his grandsons were ultimately buried in the same grave in York Cemetery.

Henry and Catharina had five surviving sons. The eldest, also called Henry, was born in 1796 and had a much-travelled army career, in the 81st Regiment. In 1826 he married Harriet Amelia Fraser, of Halifax, Nova Scotia. They had ten children and it was their second daughter, Emily Georgiana (born at St John's, New Brunswick, Canada), who married the Rev Gilbert Philips, Rector of Dringhouses. The family spent several years abroad before settling in the York area.

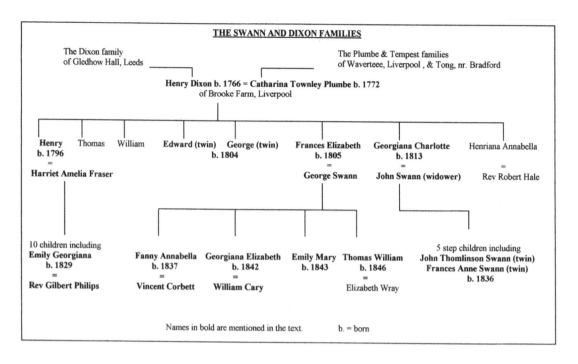

THE SWANN AND DIXON FAMILIES

The Dixon family
of Gledhow Hall, Leeds

The Plumbe & Tempest families
of Waverteee, Liverpool , & Tong, nr. Bradford

Henry Dixon b. 1766 = Catharina Townley Plumbe b. 1772
of Brooke Farm, Liverpool

Henry
b. 1796
=
Harriet Amelia Fraser

Thomas

William

Edward (twin)
b. 1804

George (twin)

Frances Elizabeth
b. 1805
=
George Swann

Georgiana Charlotte
b. 1813
=
John Swann (widower)

Henriana Annabella

=
Rev Robert Hale

10 children including
Emily Georgiana
b. 1829
=
Rev Gilbert Philips

Fanny Annabella
b. 1837
=
Vincent Corbett

Georgiana Elizabeth
b. 1842
=
William Cary

Emily Mary
b. 1843

Thomas William
b. 1846
=
Elizabeth Wray

5 step children including
John Thomlinson Swann (twin)
Frances Anne Swann (twin)
b. 1836

Names in bold are mentioned in the text.   b. = born

Two of Henry and Catharina's other sons were twins, Edward and George, born on 1 November 1804. Edward became a Commander in the Royal Navy, but apart from his appearance as a witness at Frances' marriage to George Swann and his being recorded at Ashfield in the 1851 census, he is a shadowy figure. George, on the other hand, has a very strong connection with Dringhouses and York, and we know far more about his life. He was in the army and, as was usual at the time, his career was punctuated by a series of purchased commissions as he moved up the ranks. He served in the 77th Regiment and was thus a participant in the Crimean War (1853-56), and in

Major General George Dixon's gravestone in York Cemetery. (R T Smith)

the thick of the action: he was appointed Commanding Officer in December 1854. He was made a CB (Commander of the Order of the Bath) on 5 July 1855, and was awarded various campaign medals. He became a Major General in November 1862, and this rank was most probably awarded by the Prince of Wales on George's retirement. By 1871, as recorded in the census of that year, George was living in the village of Dringhouses; his rank is given as Major General, CB, retired list, and he had a housekeeper and housemaid living in. He died aged 73 on 15 January 1878 at Gilling Lodge, Richmond, and was buried in York Cemetery.

George's horse

Considering the appalling conditions and privations experienced by the soldiers during the Crimean campaign, it is amazing that not only George but also his horse (called The Nigger) survived the ordeal. On their return to England, the horse must have been stabled and put out to graze at Ashfield, the home of George's sister Frances and her husband, for eventually the animal was buried there, near the northern boundary and some way beyond the ice-house. Its gravestone was removed to the Yorkshire Museum in 2009. Thus, unlike the guns which were captured at Sebastopol, placed on either side of Blue Bridge (near New Walk) and melted down during the Second World War, this gravestone, a most unusual link with an event of international importance, still exists. The inscription is mostly legible and some missing information can be supplied from other sources; only two figures and part of one date remain elusive. It reads: 'Here lies The Nigger aged 20 years, for ?? years faithful servant of Major Genl G Dixon, CB. He served with the 77th Regiment in the Crimea and bore his master gallantly through the battles of Alma and Inkermann and during the siege of Sebastopol. April ...'

The gravestone of Major General Dixon's horse. (York Museums Trust (Yorkshire Museum))

Another of the Dixon siblings was Frances' younger sister, Georgiana Charlotte. In 1842 she married John Swann (the aforementioned cousin of George Swann of Ashfield), of Askham Richard Hall, who was a widower 20 years older than she was. Moreover, he had five children aged ten and under by his first wife, including twins called John Thomlinson and Frances Anne. (These twins and Edward and George Dixon, the twins mentioned above, have a genetic link, as they all four have common ancestry in the 18th century.) John Swann's first wife Catherine (née Thomlinson) was buried in the churchyard at Long Marston; John and Georgiana are buried in the churchyard at Askham Richard, under the east window of the church. Like her sister Frances, Georgiana had married well, their husbands being bankers. They both lived in comfortable residences and must have had fulfilled lives, with family, domestic responsibilities and social standing.

The grave of John and Georgiana Swann in Askham Richard churchyard. (E A Smith)

The Bishop's Chair

As noted above, John Thomlinson Swann was a twin: he was the second son of John and his first wife, Catherine, née Thomlinson. He had a distinguished career in the Royal Navy, being a Lieutenant in 1858 and Commander in July 1864. From November 1860 he served on the *Harrier*, commanded by Malcolm MacGregor, during the New Zealand, or 'Maori', War; from March 1867 until his death, aged 32, on 25 April 1868 at Yokohama, he was Commander of the *Rattler*.

John's short life is commemorated not only by a wall memorial and a stained glass window in the south wall in Askham Richard church, but also by a beautiful chair, known as the Bishop's Chair, in Dringhouses church. On the back, it bears the inscription 'John Thomlinson Swann, Commander R.N. Born March 27th, 1836. Died at Yokohama, April 25th, 1868'. On the other side, in capitals along the top, are the words 'In memoriam' and at the centre, in a roundel, are the letters A and O (Alpha and Omega). On the front of the chair, in the centre, is the shield of St Edward the Confessor, which features a cross and five imaginary footless birds. Intriguingly, three sets of initials are also included: on the back of the chair TF and at the top of the arm-uprights, facing inwards, GES and EMS. The Rev Thomas Faulkner was the incumbent of Dringhouses from 1868 to 1875; Georgiana Elizabeth Swann and Emily Mary Swann were both daughters of George and Frances Swann of Ashfield and were 26 and 25 years old respectively when their cousin John died (very shortly, as it happened, after their father's death). They must have felt very close to this member of the Swann household at Askham Richard in order to have placed in their own parish church such a unique memorial.

The Bishop's Chair in Dringhouses church. (R T Smith)

The Bishop's Chair in Dringhouses church. (R T Smith)

St James' Church, Tong, near Bradford

In Tong church there are three simple but highly informative memorials to Catharina Dixon and four of her sons, but this is not the only aspect of the building which is of significance to Dringhouses people. The interior features are also of interest.

Two of the Dixon family memorials in St James' Church, Tong. (A Ramsbottom)

In 1725 Francis Barlow built a new church in Dringhouses, dedicated to St Helen (as was the chapel which it replaced). It was near the present church and adjacent to Roost Farm, but it was eventually deemed to be too small and was replaced by the present church in 1849. Some of the floor tiles of the 1725 building still remain in situ.

The loss of this building is most regrettable. It was the only Georgian church built in York, as the medieval churches were still in use and adequate, so we must look elsewhere in order to understand what the interior might have looked like. In Yorkshire, there are well-preserved Georgian interiors, notably in St Mary's Church, Whitby, and Holy Trinity, Goodramgate (now in the care of the Churches' Conservation Trust), but these are much older buildings adapted in a later period, and both of them significantly larger than the Dringhouses church. An excellent, unaltered, example of an interior of a small Georgian church is that of St James at Tong, built in 1727 by the Tempest family. It still retains the original box pews, the three-decker pulpit (with its date), the west gallery, and the squire's box pew with its fireplace.

The original floor tiles of the Georgian church, Dringhouses. (E A Smith)

The interior of St James' Church at Tong. (A Ramsbottom)

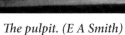

The pulpit. (E A Smith)

The squire's box pew. (M J Ramsbottom)

When a visit to Tong church in order to look at the Georgian interior led to the discovery of the Dixon wall memorials, it was one of those moments – not infrequent in family and local history research – when one is stopped in one's tracks by an amazing coincidence.

8.   *LOST HOUSES*

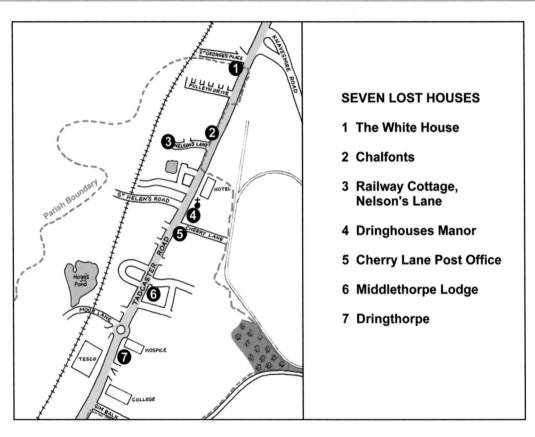

SEVEN LOST HOUSES

1 **The White House**

2 **Chalfonts**

3 **Railway Cottage,
   Nelson's Lane**

4 **Dringhouses Manor**

5 **Cherry Lane Post Office**

6 **Middlethorpe Lodge**

7 **Dringthorpe**

Sketch-map showing sites of seven lost houses in the parish of Dringhouses. (B Gaunt)

During the centuries when Dringhouses was a village of farms and smallholdings, with related trades such as carpenters, smiths and hauliers, there would have been little visible change, but after the Dringhouses Act of Enclosure in 1822 things would never be the same again. What we now know as Dringhouses Parish (formed from areas previously under the parochial care of St Mary's Bishophill Senior, Holy Trinity Micklegate, and the Parish of Acomb) stretches from St George's

Place at its northern end, to Sim Balk Lane at its southern end, and also covers farmland and Askham Bog Nature Reserve to the south-west. Of course, over the years, many more than seven houses have been lost. The seven properties selected here, which all disappeared in the mid-20th century, are of varied types, and their situation helps us understand the development of Dringhouses over a century and a half. They also highlight what has sadly been lost.

The White House

Situated on Tadcaster Road, not far from the end of St George's Place, The White House was built in the 17th century and was called New Inn on a 1731 engraving, but by 1772 John Lund's map shows it as Gallows House. Its name changed again on Francis White's map of 1785 to Tyburn House. These names are all clues as to its situation near the public gallows and its use as a place of refreshment for the crowds who enjoyed the grisly spectacle!

In the 19th century the property had a variety of uses. A Mr Thompson lived there in 1808 and the building was described as a 'starch manufactory', which had ceased to function by 1814. The various buildings which had been erected behind the property were used in the 1820s and 1840s as dog kennels. The estate map of 1838, a copy of which can be seen in St Edward's Church, shows the site as the York & Ainsty Kennels. This led to complaints from local residents about the smell of the cooking of dog food!

The White House.
(York Archives & Local History Service)

In the 1860s the property's varied use included farming, laundry and the licensed trade again. The proprietors of the inn were the owners of the Royal Station Hotel, York, but they allowed the licence to lapse and the property was divided into two houses. The Howden family used it as a dairy from the 1890s to 1939 and remained in occupation until the 1950s.

The hunt connection is confirmed by the 1841 census entry for Thomas Ecclesfield (foxhound whipper) and William Danby (huntsman) 'behind the White House'. The residents listed in 1851 are Joseph Spencer, a farmer of 20 acres, and John Shipton, a Chelsea Pensioner. Shipton would have been an 'out-pensioner' i.e. one who kept his army pension and lived at home, rather than in the Royal Hospital, Chelsea. The 1852 Ordnance Survey map shows the house with an orchard at its side, running alongside Tadcaster Road, and still surrounded by fields bounded by Hob Moor and the railway line.

An elderly Dringhouses resident recalled how local children loved to collect a jug of milk from the dairy in the 1920s, because they were amused by the *talking parrot kept on the verandah behind*

PULLEYN DRIVE
LEADING TO
WHITE HOUSE ESTATE

Although new houses have now been built on the site, The White House name is perpetuated in the estate built on the land which once surrounded the property. (R T Smith)

the house. The property was still surrounded by fields and enjoyed the view of the Knavesmire with the bandstand (opened in 1913) just across Tadcaster Road. By the time The White House was demolished in 1955, its external condition had deteriorated. However, the Royal Commission on Historical Monuments had been able to survey the property and mentioned that the interior originally had open fireplaces spanned by oak beams which were partly filled in to receive later firegrates. They also dated the staircase in the entrance hall as 18th century, and noted the first floor fireplaces with 18th- or 19th-century surrounds. Some panelling from the 17th century had also survived in the bedrooms.

Chalfonts

Situated on Tadcaster Road, where the entrance to Chalfonts cul-de-sac is now, this house was one of four villas built in the 1830s for the wealthy middle-class professionals wanting to move out of the city centre. The 1838 estate map, mentioned above, shows the plot allocated to Joseph Cooke.

1936 aerial photograph showing Chalfonts, third from the right, with its curving garden path, glasshouses, gardener's cottage, and tennis court behind. (Copyright, Blom Aerofilms)

According to directory and census records he was a gentleman of independent means. The 1839 Dringhouses Tithe Map, in the Borthwick Institute for Archives, shows his house and garden. By 1892 more villas had been erected between Chalfonts and Hob Moor.

A desirable residence, it was seen as a suitable address for families with servants, and became the residence of a Captain Heap, who moved here from Cheshire in 1863. The Heaps had connections with Alne (near Easingwold) and gave the property the name Alne Villa, changed by later residents to Alne Lodge, and finally to Chalfonts when the Quaker Rowntree family moved in. Since the 1830s the property had been home to a hat maker, army officers, a clergyman, a wealthy widow, sweet manufacturers (the Cravens) and then, for over fifty years, the chocolate manufacturing Rowntree family.

Arnold Rowntree, Liberal MP for York from 1910 to 1918, had been brought up next door (no. 302) and would see Chalfonts as an ideal family house with room to entertain. He bought the house in 1906, and Lloyd George visited the property when he was supporting Arnold Rowntree's 1910 election campaign. Students from Bootham and The Mount schools were regularly entertained here. Roger Clark, a Quaker visitor, wrote of the *pleasant outdoor lunch... about 50 in all* – so the large garden was obviously very useful!

From 1955 to 1957, it was the Officers' Mess of Headquarters Northern Command. When it was purchased in 1959 by the Shepherd building firm and the area redeveloped, its condition had deteriorated and demolition took place in 1960. Once again, we are indebted to the Royal Commission for an accurate record of the property, which tells us that it was a villa with three bays, two storeys, cellars and attics. It had brick walls and a slate roof. The exterior had been stuccoed and the windows were of a late 16th-century style. There was a glazed way to the porch, which itself had a scrolled iron balcony above it, like that still existing at no. 302. Internally, few original features remained apart from some doorcases and doors. A large two-storey extension had been added to the north side of the house.

Many Dringhouses residents remember the glass structure which covered the steps from the road up to the front door (with potted plants on the steps) although this was not an original feature, being added by the Rowntree family, possibly in 1928. Former Dringhouses church choirboys recall climbing these steps at Christmas, prior to singing in the hall and receiving a piece of fruit and a chocolate bar!

As well as the lawn just behind the house where family and friends could play croquet, the Rowntrees had purchased extra land at the rear of the property and were able to set out a tennis court where Arnold had an annual tennis match with the then Archbishop of York, William Temple. These two men were both large in size and personality (Arnold's nickname was 'Chocolate Jumbo'!) and such sporting encounters would be another instance of the fun and friendship for which Chalfonts was well known.

A modern house replaced Chalfonts after demolition, and further houses now occupy the original long garden. The house left its name to the road which eventually replaced it.

North Eastern Railway Cottage

Robert Cooper's 1832 map of Part of the Ainsty shows the brickyard close to Little Hob Moor and a new lane (now known as Nelson's Lane) which had been developed to give access to the site. As well as the main brickyard buildings at the northern end of the site, a single building is clearly marked at the Nelson's Lane end. When in use by the brickyard company, this could have originally been an office, then perhaps the manager's cottage. A long low window on one side of the building has been suggested as the place where the workmen came to collect their pay.

A railway line was built to the west of the cottage not long after the formation of the York & North Midland Railway in 1835, and the brickworks closed in 1902 when owner John Nelson became bankrupt. The North Eastern Railway Company bought the land including the cottage in 1903. Railway sidings had appeared by the 1890s and were added to over the decades which followed. The cottage was in a useful position close to the sidings for removal of waste ashes from the steam trains, and the disused claypits were used for depositing this waste. There was enough land for stabling a horse and cart, and later lorries.

No photograph survives of this humble dwelling, but its early 20th-century occupants described just two main rooms: a living room with a cooking range, and a bedroom. There was a small scullery at the rear of the cottage (with a single tap but no sink) which led to an outside toilet. The 1891 census names Charles Locking as foreman of the brickyard, so perhaps he lived in the property, and in 1901 we find Henry Oakley, a contractor's carter, living in the brickyard. The Banks family moved into the property around 1910.

The Banks family around 1918. L. to r.: Stanley, Lilian holding baby Mabel, Kitty, Arthur with Cyril on his knee, and Elsie.

(D R Reed collection)

Arthur Banks had a contract with the railway company to empty trucks full of rubbish and ashes. He also delivered coal and, like many Dringhouses families at the time, kept chickens and pigs. His daughter Elsie's reminiscences mention *one or two very nasty cockbirds which were round about the yard – if we wanted to go to the toilet, we used to peep outside to see if the cockbird was near, and if not, make a dash for the loo!* The growing family meant that a wooden extension was erected, quite close to the sidings, on the west side of the cottage to give more bedroom space. The children had a happy open-air childhood in spite of the close proximity of brickponds and railway lines.

Although the cottage was small, there were pigsties and a large granary which stored hay above the stable area below. There was a wash-house across the yard containing a little fireplace and hob, as well as the copper. In addition to being used for the washing, with water obtained from a rainwater butt, the copper was also used for boiling potatoes to feed the pigs. The children attended Dringhouses School and were escorted by their dog to make sure they got past the brickpond safely. However, life consisted of more than school and play; they had to help chop sticks and bundle them ready for sale, hold the coal bags when being filled, and help look after the animals. Elsie remembered feeding the pigs: *Sometimes we got a bit frightened of the big pig, and would just throw its food over the half-door of the sty, and hope it went into the trough!*

Her brother and father had found a stray pig which was never claimed so they were able to keep it. *We called her Bessie,* Elsie said, *blue and white she was, grew really big and was a real pet. She had 19 piglets, but one died. I was working at Terry's at the time – it was the talk of the factory – 18 piglets!* As well as the chickens and pigs, there was a vegetable garden and Mrs Banks supplemented the family income by dressmaking. She remained in the cottage after the family had all moved on, finally being rehoused when the cottage was demolished around 1958.

Dringhouses Manor

Frances Leigh (née Barlow) was the last of the Barlow family (builders of Middlethorpe Hall) who owned the manor of Dringhouses. After the death of her husband, Rev. Edward Trafford Leigh, in 1847, Frances returned to reside in Dringhouses while the new church, dedicated to St Edward the Confessor, was built in his memory. She married again in December 1851, this time to an eminent doctor from Manchester, Matthew Alexander Eason Wilkinson. Sadly, Frances died in Dringhouses the following June and had no children from either marriage. Dr Eason Wilkinson became Lord

of the Manor through his marriage to Frances and the estate remained in the Wilkinson family until it was sold after the death of Colonel G A E Wilkinson in 1941.

The original Manor House had been across the road on the present library site. However, Frances may have used the 18th-century cottage situated on the opposite side between the old church of St Helen and Cherry Lane. It was added to in the early 19th century on the north end (on the church side). It would have been a convenient home from which

Rear view of Dringhouses Manor, showing 19th-century extension on right. (J Robertson collection)

Frances could supervise both the building of the new church, opened in 1849, and the provision of a suitable vicarage for the new vicar.

The 1892 Ordnance Survey map shows the property, now designated Manor House, set in ornamental gardens with an unrestricted view over its garden and fields down to the Knavesmire. The entrance was from Tadcaster Road and in the entrance hall there was an 18th-century stone fireplace. The early 18th-century staircase is said to have been brought from a property in Bootham, along with some early 17th-century panelling in one of the rooms.

After Frances died, Dr Wilkinson remarried and continued his medical career in Manchester, but he is buried in St Edward's church grounds, with Frances and his second wife, Louisa. The property does not appear to have been used by the Wilkinson family as a regular residence prior to the 1890s. Col. George Wilkinson had inherited the manor after the death of his father and was well-known for his love of sport and horse racing.

After Col. Wilkinson's death in 1941 the house and land was sold to Frederick Welton Shepherd (of the noted building firm). He and his wife had already lived in a house on Tadcaster Road prior to making the Manor House their family home. The sale particulars, dated October 1941, describe the property as follows:

.... a charming creeper-clad well equipped Residence, brick built..... on the East side of the main York to Tadcaster Road in the delightful village of Dringhouses on the outskirts of the City of York, with spacious lawns and ornamental gardens overlooking the park land of the Home Farm.

The Manor contains the following principal rooms:- on the ground floor, Lounge Hall with tiled floor and Inner Hall, Dining Room, Drawing Room with oak parquetry floor and bay window overlooking lawns, Study. On the first floor are three principal Bedrooms fitted with handbasins in each room, Bathroom with WC, separate WC on landing.

The Domestic Offices on the ground floor include Staff Sitting Room, Larder, Back Kitchen fitted with Ideal hot water boiler, Main Kitchen adjoining with Aldwych gas oven and gas cooker, Butler's Pantry with fitted sink and store closet adjoining. Above are 2 Maids' Bedrooms, one with fixed lavatory basin, Boxroom. Wine and Coal Cellars. Air Raid Shelter with lavatory adjoining.

ELECTRIC LIGHT AND CENTRAL HEATING are fitted throughout the House. Electric light is installed in the buildings.

The Manor has a frontage to the street of approximately 285 feet. Brick and tile built Double Garage, Garden and Store House with subsidiary Heating Boiler connected to Central Heating Unit. Heated Greenhouse and Loggia.

The Vegetable Gardens adjoining are exceptionally productive and well arranged. Brick built Stables consist of 2 Two-stall Stables, 5 Large Loose Boxes, Fruit Store Room, Harness Room (now used as Laundry). The principal heated Garage, 25 ft. x 12 ft. with folding doors, Secondary Garage, 16 ft. x 12 ft., Store above 2 Garages and Loose Boxes, Small Shed housing separate heating boiler for garages. A petrol pump with filling hose and underground storage tank is installed in the stableyard.

The Shepherd family enlarged the property at the south end and the exterior walls were cased with modern brick. A comparison of their alterations with the original cottage shows the chimney stack has been raised as the roof height has been increased – this is the chimney which had been at the end of the 18th-century section of the cottage.

Although the interior was adapted for 20th-century comfort, many earlier features were retained, such as original fireplaces and some low ceilings, the tiled floor and stairs in the entrance hall, and some early panelling. F W Shepherd was Sheriff of York in 1952 and the magnificent garden was an ideal location for holding a garden party. The ancient cedar tree still remained, as did the unrestricted view down to the racecourse.

Dringhouses Manor House was demolished after 1966 when the land was sold to Trust House Forte, and the Post House Hotel was erected. Fortunately, the cedar tree was retained. The hotel is currently the Holiday Inn and the cedar tree still survives. Some reminders of the Manor House history, and its owners, are the church built here by Frances Leigh, and the library

Rear view of Dringhouses Manor after the Shepherd family's alterations. (J Robertson collection)

Garden Party held in 1952 when F W Shepherd was Sheriff of York. (Picture, The Press, York)

building (which was at one time the school she provided). The street names of Eason Road and Eason View, Dringhouses Bowling Club, the Cricket Ground and Dringhouses Cemetery all have connections with Colonel Wilkinson.

Cherry Lane Post Office

There had been a dwelling on the corner of Cherry Lane and Tadcaster Road for centuries (see Samuel Parsons' map of 1624 in section 4) with land behind it useful for market gardening. The property and land was still being used for this purpose in the 19th century. In 1839 Richard Rhodes, a gardener who came from Appleton Roebuck, was living here and after his death in 1847, his widow Elizabeth carried on the cultivation of the plot.

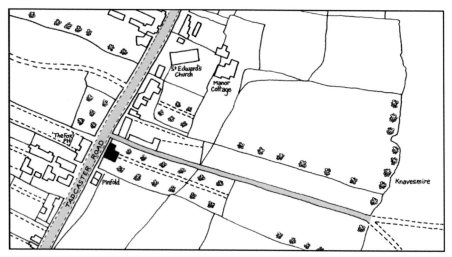

Sketch-map based on the 1852 Ordnance Survey map, showing the site between Cherry Lane and the Pinfold, with a central path stretching down the orchard garden behind it. (B Gaunt)

However, there was no post office at this stage, as in 1872 Dringhouses was still getting a post messenger from York daily. The Brown family (market gardeners) were living at the end of Cherry Lane from the 1870s, and it was a Mrs Harriet Thompson who ran a post office from her grocer's shop (possibly in Meek's Buildings across the road) in the 1880s and 1890s. The 1891 census still lists Joseph Brown as a market gardener, but by 1900 he is listed as Postmaster at the Post Office & Telegraph Office. By 1909, it was Frederick Brown whose occupation is given as provision dealer at the post office. During the 19th century, it was common to find villagers turning their front room into a shop of some sort, and this is what seems to have happened here.

Although many residents have vivid memories of the building, no complete photograph has been found to date. By 1931 Mr J W A Clark was running the post office and a 1949-50 Directory lists Mr H Hunt, who is remembered by many in Dringhouses. He was in charge of the post office counter, while Mrs Hunt, in her wrap-over pinafore, served bread and sweets at another counter. People who were children at the time all mention the *three steps up to the door* which had to be climbed prior to the purchase of their favourite sweets! Others remember Mrs Hunt selling bags of pears gathered from the large pear tree in the garden behind.

The Post Office was sold, along with Dringhouses Manor, in 1941, when it was described as a

substantial double-fronted brick-built house with slate roof together with Shop and Offices, etc., and extensive Buildings and Garden Land... having a frontage to the main road of 122 feet, in the occupation of Mr H T Hunt on an annual tenancy.... The House contains on the ground floor, Large Sitting Room, Kitchen, Retail Serving Shop and Post Office, Pantry, Offices or Storerooms, and usual Out Offices.

On the first floor are 3 Bedrooms, Bathroom and WC. The Out Buildings include 2 Loose Boxes, 3 Garages and 2 Piggeries. Electric light is installed in part of the premises by the tenant, and the lean-to corrugated iron roofed shed at the side of the house is the tenant's property.

In 1953, Mr Hunt was still running a sub-post office and selling confectionery. In 1965 he is listed as a confectioner only, the post office having moved to Ramsden's newsagents down the road opposite Walnut Cottage. The property was demolished around 1966 and new houses built on the plot.

A postcard view of the Post Office behind the Pinfold, with an early motor car parked outside.

(Dringhouses School collection)

Middlethorpe Lodge

Middlethorpe Lodge is the house which gave its name to the Middlethorpe estate at the southern end of the village, and stood where The Spinney is now. It was built for an eminent Methodist businessman, James Meek, a currier (leather manufacturer), who expanded his interests to include the Fishergate glassworks and the railway. He began buying the land in 1827 and had this elegant house built of white brick, with spacious rooms and beautiful internal features in 1836, the year he first served as Lord Mayor of York. It was accessed

Rear view of Middlethorpe Lodge from the south-east.

from Tadcaster Road and had grounds which, at various times during its existence, included conservatories, a fernery, greenhouses, an entrance lodge, stables, coach house and cottages. Its distinctive tower was a later addition, and would have provided wonderful views in all directions.

James Meek Senior   *Sir James Meek*

(Portraits reproduced courtesy of the Meek family)

The property was inherited by James Meek junior after his father's death in 1862. Like his father, James served as Lord Mayor three times, and was knighted in 1869. Family portraits show James Meek senior and his son Sir James. Both father and son played a very active part in the 19th-century York scene. Sir James sold the property to Joseph Mills in 1882 and it passed to Alfred James Bethell in 1895.

Those who remember the interior of the house recall beautiful mahogany doors, a marvellous staircase and grand fireplaces. Walter Brierley's architectural drawings, to be found in the Borthwick Institute for Archives, reveal plans for work on the house in 1907 when Sir John Grant Lawson bought it. These show the layout of the house with an entrance porch, large hall (with staircase), drawing room and dining room. Off the hall was the owner's room (study), with billiard room adjacent. There was a butler's pantry, housekeeper's room, servants' hall (with bedrooms for valet and footmen), kitchen, scullery, cleaning room and wash-house.

Sir John is remembered as a very genial character and the employer of a large staff. He was at one time MP for Thirsk & Malton and Deputy Lieutenant for the North Riding of Yorkshire. He

Memorial plaque to Sir John Grant Lawson in
St Edward the Confessor Church, Dringhouses.

(R T Smith)

married in 1902, was Deputy Speaker of the House of Commons by 1905 and was created a Baronet in December that year. The Grant Lawsons were well-known figures in Dringhouses life but Sir John died in 1919 and his widow, Lady Sylvia, would experience the problems shared by many large house owners after the First World War, trying to run a property with new constraints.

Lady Sylvia stayed there until 1930, the land then passing to property developers. Houses began to be built on the estate. During the Second World War, the house was requisitioned for Army use. After the war the closed-up house and overgrown gardens were a sad reflection of the property in its heyday. In the 1950s, the Shepherd building firm bought and built on land on 'back Middlethorpe Drive' and by 1960 they were building the properties in The Spinney where Middlethorpe Lodge had once stood.

Dringthorpe

Dringthorpe was a large late-Victorian house, built between the sale of some Ashfield land by the Swann family in 1873 and 1881, when it appears in the census returns. The Ordnance Survey map of 1909 shows the house, with its stable block and cottage (now part of St Leonard's Hospice) at right angles to the house.

It is the largest and latest of the seven lost houses. There is an obvious change of style and proportion: it had many gables and bay windows. The windows provided extra light and the gables gave the façade of the house more character. Advances in later 19th-century glass-making technology enabled larger sheets of glass to be manufactured, leading to full pane sash windows, undivided by glazing bars. The dining room had a large window overlooking the lawn. Counting the pots on the ornate chimney stacks reveals just how many fireplaces there were. According to a former resident, all the rooms (including bedrooms) had open fireplaces and marble mantelpieces. There were bells throughout the house to call servants, and the circuits for the system remained in place long after it ceased to be a private residence.

This surviving cottage and stable block give an impression of the style of the house itself, with ornate chimneys, roof tiles and bargeboards. (R T Smith)

The house had both cellars and attics, and there was access to the roof from the attics via a tiny staircase. The main entrance to the house was through a heavy double front door leading into a small lobby, and a part-glazed inner door which led into the main entrance hall, with its highly polished wooden floor. The main staircase went off the hall with a large window on

Rear façade of Dringthorpe, possibly in the 1950s. (Picture, The Press, York)

the landing. From the first floor landing, a corridor led right to the other end of the house. One of the large main bedrooms had a white marble fireplace, and there was a seat in the window above the front door, giving a view out over the drive.

The first owner of this grand house was George Oldfield, a bachelor, who retired to Dringhouses after living in Lendal where he had been involved with the family wine merchants' business all his working life. His mother, Ann, had been born in the Mansion House when her father (Thomas Wilson) was Lord Mayor in 1791. George's father, William, was the thirteenth and youngest child of Joshua Oldfield and his wife Dorothy Swann. George, in his turn, was one of sixteen children born to William and Ann! Though a bachelor himself, he had ample room to entertain his many relations.

George was a manager of Dringhouses School, and the school log book records that he paid for the re-flooring of the schoolroom (now Dringhouses Library) which took place during the 1886 Christmas holidays. He died in 1895 and the inscription on the beautiful reredos in St Edward's Church records that it was presented to the church in his memory.

Later occupants included Col. Charles John Reed in 1897, and Lieut. General Sir Laurence J Oliphant KCVO, CB. The army connection continued when First World War hero General Plumer resided there while in Northern Command. In 1919 the house was bought by William Cooper, who served as Lord Mayor of York in 1938-9. He lived there with his family until his death in 1947. By 1950 it was the Blind School Annexe and then became the Yorkshire School for the Blind from 1953 until 1965. The main house was demolished after that date and St Leonard's Hospice was built on part of the grounds. The Square, a residential development, was built on the rest in 2007-8.

MIDDLETHORPE DRIVE
LEADING TO
LYCETT ROAD, DRINGTHORPE ROAD, LAWSON ROAD, MIDDLETHORPE GROVE, WHIN CLOSE, WHIN GARTH, WHIN ROAD

The house has given its name to Dringthorpe Road, and a former owner of Middlethorpe Lodge is commemorated by Lawson Road.

(R T Smith)

The history of these seven houses illustrates many of the changes which took place in Dringhouses during the 19th century, not only in the style and development of property, but also in the type of residents it attracted. The agriculture-based society, as seen in The White House and Dringhouses Manor with its Home Farm, continued. National expansion of new housing and railways produced the brickyard/railway cottage. The increasing population of the village led to old occupations, such as market gardening, being coupled with retailing, as in the Cherry Lane Post Office. The growth in numbers of affluent middle-class businessmen who could afford larger and more impressive houses (such as Chalfonts, Middlethorpe Lodge and Dringthorpe) meant that land was required outside the city centre and led to the extension of Dringhouses towards the south. These new residents added another layer to the social structure of the village.

Although all seven properties were demolished in the 1950s and 1960s, some knowledge of them gives an increased understanding of the area, and appreciation of the special character of other unique buildings which still contribute to the identity of Dringhouses today.

9. ALDERSYDE HOUSE

In the Beginning

On 22 June 1891, Henry Ernest Leetham (known as Ernest because his father was called Henry) bought a plot of land located to the north of Moor Lane and west of Tadcaster Road. The sellers were James and William Meek and the purchase document, held in the North Yorkshire Archives at Northallerton, states that the purchase consisted of 'a parcel of land known as Leather Field (5 acres and 25 perches), a house therein called Aldersyde, plus cottages and outbuildings'.

A further purchase of land was made some years later. In 1922, the area to the north of the original plot was bought from Lady Sylvia Grant Lawson. This plot is now the area occupied by the northern part of the small development known as Aldersyde and backs onto The Horseshoe.

Ernest commissioned the architect, Walter G Penty FRIBCI, to design the house, and the initial drawings were completed in July 1894. Work commenced in 1895, although who carried out the building work is at present unknown. Although W G Penty signed the original plans of the house, the final design is attributed to his son, Arthur J Penty and it is recorded as Arthur's first important work.

This photograph of the house was taken within a few years of the house being completed because the grassed area seen here in the foreground had been transformed into a tennis court by 1910. (R Robinson collection)

Ernest retained the name Aldersyde House for his new home, the address being 144 Tadcaster Road. Access was via a driveway from Tadcaster Road.

Rear of Aldersyde House around 1905.
(Photograph probably taken by Kathleen Leetham.)
(I Robinson collection)

The House

In all the years that the house has been standing, the external appearance has changed little. However, there are three areas where changes can be easily identified.

In 1905 there was a full balcony over the back entrance plus a covered way between the house and Orangery. The balcony had been reduced and the covered way removed by the time the house had been converted to flats. The third change is that the stone cladding has been painted in recent years – originally it was left in its natural colour.

Aldersyde House in 2006. (M J Ramsbottom)

Main entrance. (M J Ramsbottom)

The main hall fireplace. (M J Ramsbottom)

The house comprises three floors and a cellar, with the main entrance on the north side. This originally led into a magnificent hall that went all the way through to the rear entrance. The hall was double height with oak-panelled walls and a superb staircase that had carvings at each turn.

However, the key feature of the hall was, and still is, a marble and alabaster fireplace complete with a signed sculpture by W G Milburn, who was also responsible for the statues of George Leeman and William Etty in York.

The sculpture by W G Milburn. (M J Ramsbottom)

Main staircase. (M J Ramsbottom)

The staircase, like the wall panels, is made of oak and the carvings are typical of the Victorian style in large houses of the day. Each piece of carving is unique and of high quality.

One quite odd feature is the little boy located by the rear entrance. Although difficult to see here in the photograph, the words 'Good Morning' are either side of his face – not, I suspect, part of the original carving but added by one of the family at some stage!

Carving of the little boy.
(M J Ramsbottom)

The dining room in 1900.

Every family room, with the exception of the dining room, still retains some of the original features of the house; unfortunately the dining room was stripped of its oak panels and fireplace in the early 1960s when the house was first converted into flats. However, a picture dating from the early 1900s shows the room in all its splendour. Above the fireplace were the words WELL BEFALL HEARTH AND HALL and the words EAST WEST HAME'S BEST appear above the main fireplace in the hall. Such mottoes were a common feature in large Victorian houses.

The Gardens, Orangery and Fernery

If the house was, and still is in part, a magnificent building, the gardens were its equal. Sadly, these began to decline at the start of the Second World War when most of the gardeners left to join up, and very little is left today.

As well as the gardens, there was an Orangery and a Fernery, the latter now being used as a workshop. However, the Orangery remains, and is now used as a communal area by the current occupants of the house.

As well as extensive walks through wooded areas, the gardens boasted two ponds and a tennis court. The ponds were connected at two points by narrow channels, the longer being through what can only be described as a small ravine.

Close to the house were formal gardens, those to the south side being rose beds surrounded by paving, some of which remains to this day in the form of a wide path across the lawn area. Originally the centrepiece of this area was a large stone boar on a plinth but this was stolen from the grounds some years ago and not recovered.

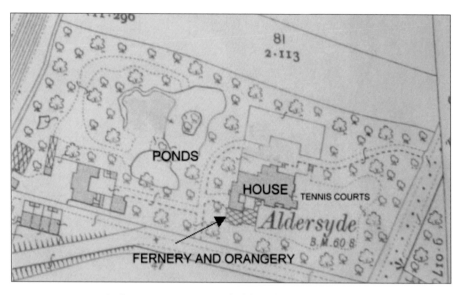

1909 Ordnance Survey map of Aldersyde House and gardens.
(York Archives and Local History Service)

The ravine was a wonderful place
for the children and this picture
was taken around 1932 when the
Robinsons and their four boys
occupied the house.

(R Robinson collection)

The larger of the ponds was of
sufficient size to enable boating to
take place.

(R Robinson collection)

There are no photographs of the Orangery as it originally was that do it justice and, in fact, by 2004 it was in a very sorry state. Since then attempts have been made to bring it back to a reasonable condition and the results can be seen below. The marble urn is an original feature; unfortunately it is in poor condition.

The Orangery in 2010. Vines, a fig tree and a passionflower are all flourishing. (A Ramsbottom)

The Orangery in 2004. (M J Ramsbottom)

The Outbuildings

As well as the house and gardens, there were stables and a cottage, in which lived the head groom. Mr Shorney, who is named as occupying this post in the 1901 census, remained with the family for many years and eventually became chauffeur.

The cottage and stables still exist down Old Moor Lane and have been converted into apartments.

The stables around 1910. (I Robinson collection)

The Leethams

The Leetham family was the first of the two families who occupied Aldersyde House in its first 60 years.

Ernest Leetham was born in 1861, the third son of Henry and Mary Leetham. Three of his uncles were master mariners, as were their father and grandfather before them. His own father, Henry, made his name by founding the firm of Henry Leetham & Sons, Millers of York and introducing the use of rolling mills to grind flour – a system he acquired from the Netherlands that was far more efficient at producing flour than the use of grindstones.

Although it was Ernest's eldest brother who succeeded his father as chairman of the company, Ernest was fully involved in transforming it into one of York's leading companies of the day. He was clearly a very astute businessman. Ernest married Mary Hannah Coning (Minnie), the only daughter of Thomas Coning by his first marriage.

Thomas was a councillor as well as shopkeeper at a property on Blossom Street. When Thomas' second wife died in 1883, Minnie took on the responsibility of bringing up her six young half-siblings, a duty she took so seriously that for a while she turned down all Ernest's advances! However, they were eventually married shortly after her 22nd birthday in 1885.

Minnie and Ernest's engagement photo. They married in 1885.

(A Robinson collection)

Ernest's business acumen not only played its part in the development of the mills, but in time was a major factor in turning around Joseph Terry & Sons into a successful chocolate company. He was Chairman of that company from 1915 until his death in 1923, the first non-Terry to hold the post. Ernest was Sheriff of York between 1912-1913, a post previously held by his father in the 1890s; this was the first time that both a father and son had served in that office in the city. He was also a governor of the Merchant Adventurers from 1915 to 1919.

Minnie died in 1920 and Ernest, having suffered ill health for some time, died in 1923.

Ernest and Minnie had three daughters, a fourth child dying at birth. Kathleen, Constance (Consie) and Ethel were five, nine and twelve years old respectively when they moved into Aldersyde House with their parents in 1898.

Kathleen married Noel Terry in 1915 and there is a picture of the happy couple taken in the Orangery following their marriage ceremony at Dringhouses Church. Noel and Kathleen built Goddards in 1927 and Noel had his study positioned to enable him to see Terry's factory where he had taken over the position of chairman.

Consie married Noel's older brother, Joseph Edward Harold Terry, known as Harold, also in 1915. Consie obtained a Degree in Medicine and became a lecturer at the School of Medicine for Women, London. Her husband Harold was not interested in the chocolate business but instead went into the theatre. He wrote a book called *A Fool to Fame* that sought to disprove that it was Dick Turpin who rode from London to York, and was also the co-author of a very successful play – *The Man Who Stayed at Home* – that had a run on the London stage.

Kathleen, Consie and Ethel around 1912.
(A Robinson collection)

Ethel was the eldest of Ernest and Minnie's children. During the First World War she was Commandant of the Training College, Voluntary Aid Detachment Hospital, York, and for this work she was awarded the MBE. In 1921 Ethel married Major Francis Aidan Robinson, known as Aidan, a doctor in the Royal Army Medical Corps. Aidan left the Army in 1926 and became a director of Joseph Terry and Sons. Ethel and Aidan moved into Aldersyde House after their wedding and Ernest was in the process of purchasing a house from the Terry family at the time of his death. Ernest left Aldersyde House in trust to his three daughters and Ethel remained there, paying rent to the trust, until 1957. She eventually moved to The Beeches on Tadcaster Road to be closer to her sister Kathleen, who was living next door at Goddards, and remained there until shortly before she died in 1978, aged 91.

The Robinsons

During their 30 years at Aldersyde House, Ethel and Aidan raised four sons, Francis, Michael (Mikey), Ian and Carins. The boys had a wonderful childhood there, particularly in the pre-war years, according to Ian, the only surviving member of the family at the time of writing (2010).

Both Francis and Mikey served their country during the Second World War. Francis won the Military Cross whilst Mikey was killed towards the end of hostilities. After the war Francis and Carins took up farming, whilst Ian qualified as a doctor.

Ian's claim to fame is that in 1953 he took part in an air-sea rescue from Royal Naval Station, Yeovilton – the first doctor ever to fly in a helicopter on such a mission.

Ian, Mikey, Ethel, Francis, Aidan and Carins in 1944,
photographed on the steps of Aldersyde House. (R Robinson collection)

After the Robinsons

In 1957 the house and grounds were sold by the estate agent Bernard Thorpe and Partners by direction of the Midland Bank acting on behalf of the family. The sale took place in The Royal Station Hotel on Thursday 11 April 1957. Originally the estate agents had estimated the value at between £8,000 and £10,000 and, prior to the sale, the Institute for the Deaf had shown an interest in purchasing the house and grounds. However, other correspondence indicates that 'builders had already indicated a willingness to pay £12,500' and thus it was that builders Robert Alexander Cattle of 7 Blake Street and Jack Yates, City Builder, bought the property for that amount.

By the time of the sale, the gardens were in poor condition, having been much neglected since the Second World War. Cattle and Yates built houses on the land and all that remains of the wonderful gardens are a few trees, the best preserved being a cedar tree that still stands where the gardens were.

A second sale took place to dispose of the house contents no longer required. Throughout his life Ernest had been an astute collector as a means of investment and Ethel had kept most of these items locked away in two of the rooms. It was now that many of these items went under the hammer. In total some 435 items were listed for sale. The cheapest sale item identified from the catalogue was for two Gladstone bags that went for one shilling, and the most expensive was an Italian School painting *Rocky Landscape and Figures* that sold for £195.

The cedar tree in Aldersyde. (E A Smith)

Shortly after the original sale, Cattle and Yates agreed to sell the house and a small parcel of land to Henry Gorwood. Henry converted the house into flats that were rented out until 2005 when Aldersyde Estates Ltd purchased the building and carried out a complete and sympathetic refurbishment of the flats.

Aldersyde House in 2010. (M J Ramsbottom)

10. THE BRICKWORKS' LEGACY

Travelling through Dringhouses today, by rail along the main line south out of York station or by car along Tadcaster Road, there is little obvious evidence of earlier occupations in what was essentially a separate village until after the First World War. However, for those who have time to stop and wander around the area, there are clues to the various brickworks which flourished here for well over a hundred years in the 19th and early 20th centuries. In fact, we know that the industry existed in Dringhouses as early as the 14th century, as reference is made to a 'tiler' in the Poll Tax return of 1379.

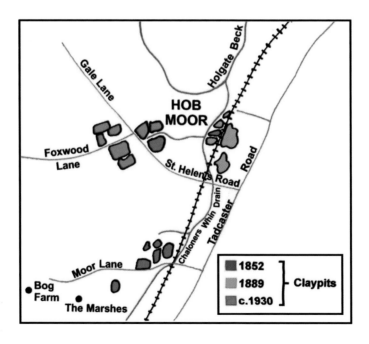

Sketch-map of 19th- and 20th-century brickworks locations. (E A Smith, adapted)

Claypits are shown on several plans and maps over this period, revealing their locations between the Hob Moor area in the north, across to the west around the present Gale Lane/Foxwood Lane junction, and along Moor Lane in the south. As these pits were gradually exhausted, they were usually filled in (reference is made to this in the 'Lost Houses – Railway Cottage' section) and in some cases the land was later built upon. Some of the ponds were allowed to fill with water and became popular sites for local anglers or other recreational use. Kelsey's Pond, which was lost in the 1950s, had been a pit from the North Field Brick Works, close to where the Edmund Wilson Swimming Baths were later built on Thanet Road. Its popular name referred to Mr Harry Kelsey who lived close by the pond and was known for pulling out the weed from the pond with a large hook. It was used by some for swimming, as well as being good for fishing and wildlife. Local angler Frank Oates was prompted to write to the *Yorkshire Evening Press* in January 1966 when Leetham's Pond on Moor Lane was threatened with being used as a refuse tip. He reminded readers that Kelsey's Pond had once been *a little jewel, full of wildlife and a joy to all who used it*, and bemoaned the loss of such ponds which had been filled in, describing them all as *little beauty spots that should have been preserved for local people to enjoy.*

A 1940s view of Kelsey's Pond, later filled in, showing its proximity to the end of North Lane.
(R T Smith collection)

Census returns and street directories give details of brickmakers in Dringhouses, particularly in the 1860s and 1870s when demand for bricks was high. References in the 1880s include the Simpsons who had a yard at Dringhouses Moor, and the Nelsons who had works in the Hob Moor area. Later reference is made to the Acomb Moor Brick Works in the 1930s. Old bricks found locally, along with street names in the area, are tantalising clues to the existence of these businesses. The last of these was Acomb Moor Brick Works, working the site on the corner of what is now Foxwood Lane and Gale Lane, which closed around 1945. Fortunately, Michael Bailey was able to interview some of the men who had worked there, and record their memories.

A Simpson's brick from the Moor Lane works and an Acomb Moor brick made in the Thanet Road area, exhibited at the Dringhouses Local History Group Heritage Morning, 21 June 2008. (R T Smith)

Acomb brickworkers in 1929. (M Bailey collection)

There is little remaining evidence of the buildings connected with the brickwork sites. 19th-century houses in Vernon Street and Rutter Street, erected on the redundant brickyard area of Little Hob Moor (once known as Brick Garth), were demolished in the early 1970s. However, a group of five houses, built around 1890, remains at the northern end of the present Hob Moor Terrace. The Nelson's Lane railway cottage, referred to above, was thought by the Banks family to have been on the site of, or an adaptation of, a brickworks building, but this was demolished in the 1950s. The Beagle public house on Foxwood Lane was originally the home of Ernie Chestney (with a 't') of the Acomb Moor Brick Works, Chesney Fields being a reference to him. The eight brickyard cottages which stood on the site of Clay Place, just beyond Chesney Fields on Gale Lane, have not survived. However, the home of Sidney Hare, a former manager of the Acomb works, still survives across the road, and is currently known as The Old Surgery. The manager's house of the Moor Lane brickworks, later the site of Leetham's Pond, also known as Hogg's Pond, had been built within the workings and became submerged when the claypit filled up with water. This pond took its name from the Leetham family of Aldersyde who once owned the land, and it later became associated with Mr Hogg, who lived close by.

Nelson's Lane refers to Thomas and John Nelson who owned brickworks at the south end of the Hob Moor site prior to 1903, and Chesney Fields commemorates Ernie Chestney of the Acomb Moor Brick Works.
(R T Smith)

So what can we actually see today on the former brickwork sites? In dry weather, the outline of the foundations of the Vernon and Rutter Street houses can be seen in the grass of Little Hob Moor, just beyond the end of Hob Moor Terrace. Today, a very pleasant, winding walk from this northern end of the former Hob Moor Brick Works leads through to Nelson's Lane and is part of the Mayfield Nature Reserve. The tranquil scene and lively birdsong are quite a contrast to the exhausting activity and heat of the industry which filled the area over a century ago! The variety of trees here includes field maple, hawthorn, willow, pine, birch, oak, ash, alder and spindle, alongside wild roses, brambles and an area of native wild flowers. These attract and support a variety of insects and birds, and together provide a valuable wildlife habitat.

Mayfield Nature Reserve and Pond, which can be accessed via Little Hob Moor, Nelson's Lane and Aintree Court. Over the years, this pond has also been referred to as Nelson's Pond and Railway Pond. (R T Smith)

Crossing over Nelson's Lane, where little evidence remains of most of the several claypits once in this area, there is a wooded approach to Mayfield Pond. This is the one remaining claypit, now much reduced in area but surrounded by trees and natural vegetation. It is a very popular venue for local anglers, with its stock of tench, roach, bream, perch and eels. Walkers might catch a glimpse of dragonflies, birds such as a kingfisher, heron, or woodpecker, and even a fox, but it is the anglers who have the best opportunities to observe the variety of wildlife here!

The icy surface of Leetham's/Hogg's Pond, viewed from Moor Lane bridge, February 2010. In the severe winter of 1947 not only was the ice thick enough to support many local skaters, but even the weight of two horses from Chapmans' farm nearby as they strayed on to it!

(R T Smith)

Leetham's Pond (now owned by York Lakeside Lodges) was once a claypit from the Moor Lane Brick Works. It is not accessible to the public but can be seen from Moor Lane bridge, and is another area beneficial to wildlife in the midst of suburban housing. Further along Moor Lane is Chapman's Pond, another flooded brick pit, which is open to the public and is also a popular site for local anglers. Surrounded by trees, with paths through grassy areas full of shrubs and wild flowers, this site is a valuable habitat for waterfowl and a variety of birds.

Not only does this pond have a similar variety of fish to that of Mayfield Pond, it is also a location where one can see almost a hundred different species of flowering plants, including tufted vetch, lady's smock, goat's-beard and red bartsia. These in turn attract butterflies including the common blue, ringlet and gatekeeper. Over the seasons the pond is used by tufted duck, great crested grebe, mallard and moorhens, and attracts dragonflies such as the brown hawker which appreciates well-vegetated ponds. Many small birds, including the willow warbler, blackcap and long-tailed tit, breed in the surrounding trees and scrub, and bats can be seen hunting over the water at dusk.

Angler at Chapman's Pond. Access is via the small car park, between Chaloners Road and what was the New Penny Stores. (R T Smith)

A tantalising glimpse of the windpump on the southern side of Moor Lane, also on private land, reminds us of the brickworks which were operated here in 1838 by Richard Dalton. This pond has sometimes been referred to as Piercy's Pond, probably a reference to Mr Piercy of Nova Scotia cottage, who farmed land in this area. The windpump is shown on the 1852 Ordnance Survey map covering the Moor Lane brickworks, and this is all that remains today. It would have had sails similar to a windmill and operated a water pump to keep the clay workings dry. Claypits in Dringhouses used these windpumps and they can be seen marked on maps as late as the 1930s, although this one off Moor Lane is the only remaining example.

Late Springtime at Chapman's Pond. (R T Smith)

Although this windpump and the few houses with connections to the brickmaking past of Dringhouses are the only original buildings which remain, we have the wonderful legacy of some of the sites and former claypits which are now valuable as wildlife habitats and recreational areas. To echo Frank Oates' words, they are, after all, little beauty spots which have been preserved for local people to enjoy and now form an important part of our green, rather than industrial, heritage.

Windpump and pond. (M Bailey)

11. DRINGHOUSES CEMETERY

The 19th-century Wilkinson grave. (R T Smith)

Dringhouses Cemetery, opened in 1927. (R T Smith)

Unlike many village churches, St Edward the Confessor, Dringhouses does not have a graveyard adjacent to it. The only burials in its grounds are those of the family who were Lords of the Manor. The 18th-century church of St Helen (replaced in the 1840s by the present church of St Edward the Confessor) contained the remains of members of the Barlow family. Later members of the family who are buried in a plot near to the end of the adjacent church hall include Frances Barlow, her second husband Dr Matthew Eason Wilkinson, and his second wife Louisa.

So where were the village residents buried before the opening of the present cemetery in Dringhouses? Some would be buried in St Mary Bishophill Senior, as part of Dringhouses was included in that parish prior to 1853, while others could be buried in York Cemetery after it opened in 1837. James Meek, who lived in Middlethorpe Lodge, Tadcaster Road, was one of the trustees of York Cemetery, which opened when the churchyards in the City were full. James and some of his descendants are buried in York Cemetery, along with several other 19th-century Dringhouses residents.

Dringhouses Cemetery was opened at the southern end of the parish in 1927, on a site between Tadcaster Road and the railway line at Chaloners Whin. Samuel Parsons' map of the Manor of Dringhouses (1624) shows that this area was part of the very long West Field, all of which was being cultivated in strips. The ridges and furrows could still be seen in the adjacent field when an aerial survey was made in 1936-7. When the rail line from York to Selby was opened in 1871, it branched off the main line at Chaloners Whin Junction and cut through the area of Sim Hills. In so doing, it swept through the field boundaries, creating the triangular shape of the site we see today. When the York to Selby line was closed in 1983, the disused railway track was made into a cycleway.

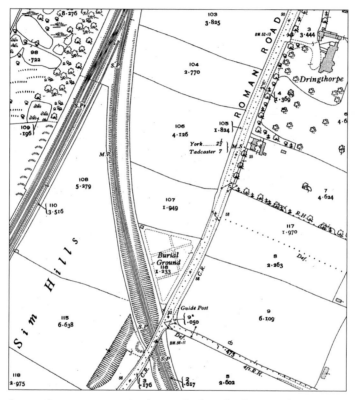

Part of the 1931 Ordnance Survey map, revised 1929 (reduced), showing the Dringhouses Burial Ground. (York Archives and Local History Service)

The land was given by Colonel Wilkinson, the last Lord of the Manor. He and his wife Caroline are both buried here – hers was actually the first burial (in 1929) in the cemetery. The square plot which contains their graves is surrounded by yew hedging, but sadly their memorial inscriptions are quite difficult to read. A similar plot is that of members of the Terry family (Noel, Kathleen and their sons Kenneth and Richard) who had lived at Goddards (now the National Trust Yorkshire Regional Office). Immediately to the right of the Wilkinson plot there is a cruciform coped gravestone, with an inscription around its edges, which is the last resting place of Dr Evelyn, the well-known York doctor who collected views of York in the early decades of the 20th century. Colonel Wilkinson and Dr Evelyn were both educated at Charterhouse in the 1870s.

Grave of William Arthur Evelyn MA MD who died 6 January 1935. Wilkinson plot to left. (R T Smith)

Some well-known Dringhouses residents, however, are not in this cemetery as might have been expected. Arnold Rowntree, York's MP from 1910 to 1918, lived at Chalfonts on Tadcaster Road, but was buried in the Quaker Meeting House grounds, Pickering, when he died in 1951. His father, John Stephenson Rowntree, who had lived at No. 302 Tadcaster Road (currently the Knavesmire Manor Hotel) from the 1860s, was buried in the Quaker Burial Ground, Heslington Road, when he died in 1907. Some residents who died before the provision of Dringhouses Cemetery are buried in Bishopthorpe churchyard. These include Sir John Grant Lawson, once the Deputy Speaker of the House of Commons and owner of Middlethorpe Lodge from 1907, who died in 1919, and architect Walter Brierley, a former churchwarden at St. Edward's and designer of Goddards for the Terry family, who died in 1926.

A walk around Dringhouses Cemetery provides an interesting exercise. Present-day Dringhouses residents reading some of the inscriptions on the headstones will find many familiar names. Some will remember Bert Keech, the larger-than-life dance band leader and bowls champion. Others might remember Canon Lee, who gave his name to the secondary school in Clifton and was Rector of Holy Trinity, Micklegate from 1927 until he retired in 1947. An interesting square plot laid out in brick is a fitting indication of the professional history of members of the Shepherd building family buried here. Charles Minter, the York City Engineer and Planning Officer from 1935 to 1962, is also remembered with respect by many.

Memorials to Bert Keech (left) and Canon Lee (right). (R T Smith)

84

The memorial to the Grisdale family is a reminder of John and Jessie who owned the fondly remembered ladies' outfitters in Coney Street, on the site later taken over by W H Smith. They had a large house, named Tollgarth, built on Tadcaster Road opposite the junction with Hunters Way. There is a stained glass window in memory of them in St Edward the Confessor Church.

Grisdale family headstone. (R T Smith)

Looking at the memorial inscriptions, the reader begins to wonder at the stories behind some of the people here. There is the poignant record of 21-year-old Flt. Sgt. Malcolm M Stembridge, a pilot who was killed in action in Germany in 1944. Then there is a touching reminder of husband and wife James and Elizabeth Lofthouse, who lived into their eighties and died within days of each other. A more mysterious inscription just reads 'Til minde om min elskede mand, Harold' which could indicate a Norwegian connection. Another enigma is the headstone engraved with bars of music, which are now so eroded that its tune must remain silent. There are many people here who survived to a good old age, with more than fifty in their eighties, and several in their nineties, one even reaching 99. This must be a recommendation for living in Dringhouses! Since 1937 the cemetery, containing 743 plots, has been administered by the city council. It now contains an area for cremated remains as at present no new graves are available here.

12. LEST WE FORGET

Dringhouses War Memorial. (E A Smith)

During 1919, various Dringhouses people put forward ideas for the commemoration of those men from the village who had lost their lives during the First World War, 1914-18. After some debate, the war memorial which stills stands in the church grounds, at the centre of Dringhouses, was created. Designed by Walter Brierley, it is of Portland stone and has the sculpted figures of Christ, Saint George and Saint Edward at the top of the column. The names of the fallen are inscribed on a panel at the base, facing the main road and looking down St Helen's Road. The service of dedication was held on 1 October 1922, when the memorial was unveiled by the Earl of Harewood (who also gave the address) and dedicated by the Lord Bishop of Beverley; Colonel Wilkinson laid a wreath 'in the name of the Parish of Dringhouses'. In his address, the Earl of Harewood drew attention to the fact that about 200 Dringhouses parishioners went to serve with the forces and that the 29 who lost their lives represented a large percentage of that total. The table included opposite, based on research carried out by George and Daphne Robson, gives brief details of those killed.

FIRST WORLD WAR

NAME	REGIMENT/SERVICE	WHERE BURIED OR COMMEMORATED	DATE OF DEATH	AGE
Gunner A Bishop	Royal Garrison Artillery	Locre Hospice Cemetery, Belgium	2.10.1917	36
Sapper H S Brown	Royal Engineers	York Cemetery	12.9.1916	35
Corporal R M Bustard	Northumberland Fusiliers	Etaples Military Cemetery, France	17.7.1916	19
Lance Corporal T W Carlton	Northumberland Fusiliers	Arras Memorial, France	5.6.1917	?
Corporal H Clark	1st Btn West Yorkshire Regiment	Maroc British Cemetery, France	26.8.1917	38
Private T E Clark	Royal Army Service Corps	Mazargues War Cemetery, Marseilles, France	6.2.1919	22
Private J Clarkson	10th Btn Cheshire Regiment	Ypres (Menin Gate) Memorial, Belgium	11.6.1917	19
Lance Corporal C Cruse	2nd Btn Duke of Wellington's Regiment	Ypres (Menin Gate) Memorial, Belgium	11.11.1914	?
Major A H Cuthell	9th Btn West Yorkshire Regiment	Helles Memorial, Turkey	22.8.1915	36
Signaller F M Dawson	Royal Garrison Artillery	Tincourt New British Cemetery, France	5.10.1918	32
Private W Elton	1st/5th Btn West Yorkshire Regiment	De Cusine Ravine British Cemetery, France	9.1.1917	23
Private W Flanagan	12th Btn West Yorkshire Regiment	Loos Memorial, France	26.9.1915	32
Lance Corporal H Foxton	2nd Btn West Yorkshire Regiment	Ypres (Menin Gate) Memorial, Belgium	31.7.1917	24
Rifleman R W Fowler	11th Btn King's Royal Rifle Corps	Cambrai Memorial, Louverval, France	30.11.1917	20
Private A Gatus	7th Btn East Yorkshire Regiment	Arras Memorial, France	26.3.1918	26
Private O G Harris	Army Service Corps	Durban (Ordnance Rd) Military Cemetery, South Africa	13.12.1916	39
Private H Lewis	18th Queen Mary's Own Hussars	Ypres (Menin Gate) Memorial, Belgium	24.5.1915	24
Major D P Mackay	5th Btn West Yorkshire Regiment	Tyne Cot Memorial, Belgium	9.10.1917	34
Boy A Maddison	Royal Navy : HMS Hawke	Portsmouth Naval Memorial	15.10.1914	16
Private G W Mannall	7th Btn EastYorkshire Regiment	Arras Memorial, France	9.5.1917	20
Corporal F H Pfluger	27th Btn East Riding Yeomanry	Mikra Memorial, Greece	15.4.1917	27
Driver J Priest	Royal Field Artillery	York Cemetery	30.9.1915	32
Lance Corporal F C Richardson	3rd King's Own Hussars	Ypres (Menin Gate) Memorial, Belgium	30.10.1914	25
Corporal H Richardson	18th Queen Mary's Own Hussars	La Ferté-Sous-Jouarre Cemetery, France	24.8.1914	24
Lance Corporal A Shaw	24th Btn Northumberland Fusiliers	Tyne Cot Memorial, Belgium	23.10.1917	26
Private T Tate	9th Btn Northumberland Fusiliers	Ploegsteert Memorial, Belgium	25.9.1918	22
Private C Walker	9th Btn West Yorkshire Regiment	Chatby Cemetery, Alexandria, Egypt	21.11.1915	22
Private F W Waudby	2nd/5th Btn Northumberland Fusiliers	York Cemetery	17.9.1919	33
Painter E Woodall	Royal Navy : HMS Cullist	Portsmouth Naval Memorial	11.2.1918	24

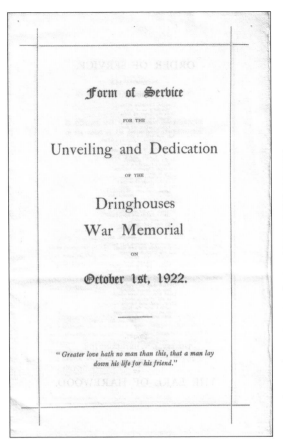

The front cover of the order of service.
(G and D Robson collection)

The First World War names and inscription.
(R T Smith)

Dringhouses parishioners killed on active service during the Second World War. These names were inscribed as the result of an initiative taken by Peter Rhodes. (R T Smith)

In the same way that the large majority of the Dringhouses servicemen killed in action in the First World War found their last resting place far from home, so did those killed in the Second World War: only one out of the six whose names are carved on the war memorial is interred in Dringhouses Cemetery. The world-wide dispersal of the other five reflects the global nature of this second terrible conflict.

All the six men who are commemorated for their sacrifice during the Second World War have living relatives. The information about each which follows has been garnered from personal reminiscences of family and friends, from newspaper articles, national and local registers and reference works. The degree of detail varies from person to person; more information will always be welcomed.

Cyril Banks

Cyril Banks was born on 15 February 1915, the son of Arthur and Lilian Banks who lived at the bottom of Nelson's Lane. There is more information about this family in section 8.

Cyril was a driver in the Royal Army Service Corps; he was a Supplementary Reservist and was called up at the outbreak of the war. Having been evacuated from Dunkirk in late May/early June 1940, he was subsequently sent to the Far East, where Japan was rapidly expanding its empire. Cyril was posted missing on 16 March 1942 and was taken prisoner; he died aged 28 on 24 November 1943, on the Burma-Siam Railway. This notorious railway was a Japanese project conceived in response to the need for improved communications to support their large army in Burma. Work began in October 1942 and its 424km (265 miles) were completed in December 1943, shortly after Cyril died. The railway was built in conditions of extreme privation by Commonwealth, Dutch and American prisoners of war, together with some conscripts and forced labour.

Cyril Banks boating on the River Ouse, 18 June 1941. (D R Reed collection)

Cyril was buried in Kanchanaburi War Cemetery, 130km (80 miles) north-west of Bangkok, Thailand, where 5084 Commonwealth casualties of the Second World War are buried or commemorated.

Gordon Cranston

Gordon Cranston was born in York in 1920 and although his younger brother and sister were born in Newcastle, the Cranston family was back in York and living in North Lane during the Second World War. Gordon was a very keen cyclist and, on his racing bike specially made for him by Elsegood's cycle shop in Lowther Street, he would do a 25-mile round trip to the other side of Tadcaster and back in just over an hour. Together with his brother John and several other young men from Dringhouses, Gordon worked at the firm of Cooke, Troughton and Simms. This famous and much-respected York firm manufactured precision instruments and made an important contribution

The 460 Squadron memorial at Binbrook, Lincolnshire.
(J M Tyszka)

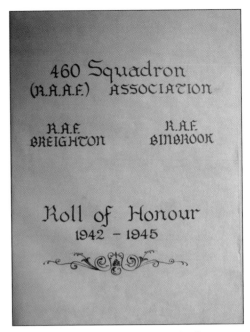

The Roll of Honour in the church of St Mary and St Gabriel, Binbrook: title page.
(J M Tyszka)

The grave of Gordon Cranston and his fellow crew, Appenwihr, February 2010. (A Ford)

to the war effort. Those working there had 'reserved occupation' status and could only leave in order to join the forces. This Gordon did: he became a sergeant in the Royal Air Force Volunteer Reserve. After six months' training in Canada, he flew Lancaster bombers with 460 Squadron (Royal Australian Air Force). 460 Squadron was originally at the heavy bomber base at Breighton, near Selby, but moved to Binbrook, Lincolnshire, on 14 May 1943; it remained there until 28 July 1945 and during that time was the sole operational unit at that base. Thus it was from Binbrook that Gordon took off at 9.32pm on 27 April 1944 as Navigator in his Lancaster,

Gordon and Helen Cranston: their wedding photograph. (C Pidd collection)

destination Friedrichshafen, on what was only his third operation. His aircraft was shot down by a German night-fighter and crashed in Eastern France, very near the German border. All seven members of the Lancaster crew were killed; they were buried in the village cemetery at Appenwihr, 9km (5 miles) south-east of Colmar. The grave is marked by three inscribed RAF headstones and a twisted propeller-blade.

Gordon was 23 years old when he died on 27/28 April 1944. On 10 November 1943, when he was home on leave, he had married Helen Roustoby, of Holgate (now Wilton) Rise, in Dringhouses church. He is remembered by Helen's sister as being well-mannered and good-looking.

William Norman Franklin

William Franklin was born in 1899 in Newcastle, to Elizabeth and William John Franklin. He married Vera, a daughter of James and Mary Snowball who in 1901 were living in Northfield Terrace; by the Second World War the Snowball family was established in Mayfield Grove.

William had served for 21 years as a Marine, had come out of the Navy and was working as a postman in York when he was called up again into the Marines just before the Second World War started. He was trained to work on DEMS (Defensively Equipped Merchant Ships), and was lost at sea, aged 41, on 11 September 1940. He was on a merchant cargo vessel, the SS *Benavon*, about 500km (300 miles) south-west of the island of Réunion in the Indian Ocean, en route from Hong Kong to the UK via South Africa carrying hemp and rubber. At this stage of the war, a convoy system for the Indian Ocean had not yet been put in place. Thus it would seem that the *Benavon* was alone when it was detected by the German auxiliary cruiser, or raider, the *Pinguin*. This vessel would have been camouflaged as an Allied or neutral ship. The practice was for the raider to approach any ship, drop the camouflage at the last instant, hoist the German flag and then fire across the ship's bows in order to stop it. The response of the *Benavon*

William Franklin with the family dog, Bud, in about 1940.

(J Fry collection)

must have been to follow Admiralty orders and broadcast 'Raider' signals, thus causing the *Pinguin* to open fire directly: the *Benavon* sank, with 23 of its complement of 48 being lost. After such an incident, Allied cruisers or hunter groups were sent to attack the German raider, and in May 1941 the *Pinguin* fell victim to British cruisers.

William Franklin is commemorated on the Plymouth Naval Memorial, which is of the same design as the one at Portsmouth (illustrated below). His name is also included on the plaque inside the entrance of the main post office in Lendal, York.

The commemorative plaque in the post office building, Lendal, York. (M J Ramsbottom)

William Alwyn Kell

William Kell, known in the family as Will, was born in 1912. The Kell family lived in The Horseshoe for a long period and many local people remember Will's father, Fred, a very well-known York musician: he revived the York Symphony Orchestra in 1933 (in Exhibition Hall) and was for a long time musical director (or leading violin, as required) at the York Empire, now the Grand Opera House. Will's brother Reginald was the internationally-renowned clarinettist and taught Benny Goodman the classical style of playing the clarinet. Will himself was solo clarinettist in the London Symphony Orchestra before the war.

During the war, Will was a Leading Seaman in the Royal Navy. He was on the SS *Selvistan* on 5 May 1943, in convoy ONS.5, 850 km (530 miles) north-east of St John's, Newfoundland. It was en route to Halifax, Nova Scotia, in order to bring back supplies to the UK, but in the late evening the convoy was attacked by the greatest number of U-boats ever employed against a single convoy. Six of the submarines were sunk but the *Selvistan*, together with other ships in the convoy, was torpedoed and sunk by U-boat 266. One crew member – Will Kell – and five gunners were lost (Will died of his wounds in the lifeboat). The 40 survivors were picked up by HMS *Tay* and landed at St. John's. Will was 30 years old. He is commemorated on the Portsmouth Naval Memorial, which comprises an obelisk and wall. The obelisk with inscribed bronze plaques around its base was erected after the First World War; the long curved wall

The Portsmouth Naval Memorial, Clarence Drive, Southsea, Portsmouth. (E A Smith)

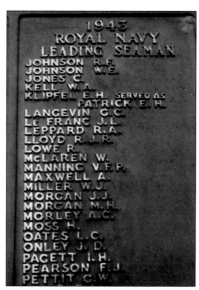

W A Kell, panel 37, column C.
(E A Smith)

Panel 37. (E A Smith)

bearing 54 similar plaques was added on the landward side after the Second World War. The names are of personnel lost at sea who have no known grave, and are arranged according to the year of death and, within each year, according to service and rank.

Will Kell (on the left) and his brother Reginald in the back garden of the family home in The Horseshoe.
(B and B Scorfield collection)

Michael Henry Aidan Robinson

Michael Robinson's initial grave.
(I Robinson collection)

Many Dringhouses people remember Mrs Robinson, Michael's mother, when she was living at The Beeches (now the Curzon Lodge Hotel) next to Goddards, but she and her husband, Major Robinson, brought up their family of four sons at Aldersyde House. (More details about the Robinson family can be read in section 9 of this book.)

As Lieutenant Robinson, 1st Battalion, Rifle Brigade, Michael took part in the Allies' forcing of the Rhine in March 1945. From the D-Day landings on 6 June 1944, the Allies had reached the point where, between 23 March and 2 April, the Second British Army was advancing north-eastwards from the Rhine towards the River Ems. It was on 1 April that, during this advance, the vehicle in which Michael and his driver were travelling hit a mine, near Ochtrup. Both were killed instantly. Michael was buried close to the place where he died by a padre from the Fifth Tank Regiment and in July 1947 was reburied in the British War Cemetery in Reichswald Forest, Kleve, about 27km (16 miles) south-east of Arnhem. He died aged 21, less than six weeks before the end of the war in Europe. He was a great sportsman and well-respected by both officers and men.

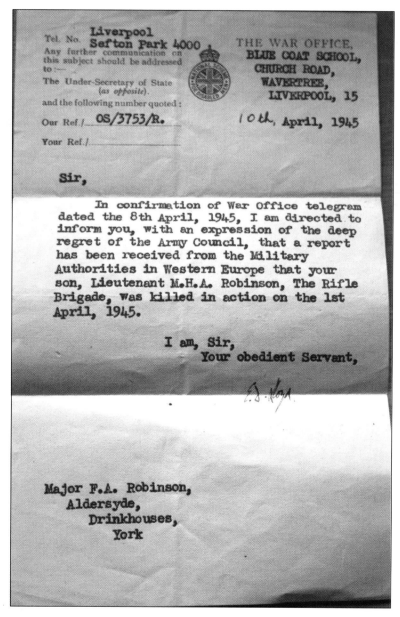

The letter to Major Robinson confirming his son's death. (I Robinson collection)

Kenneth Thomas Peart Terry

Kenneth Terry. (B Lawrie collection)

Kenneth Terry was born on 6 October 1920, the second son of Noel and Kathleen Terry, of Terry's chocolate firm. He was educated at Marlborough College and RAF College, Cranwell, and was commissioned in December 1939, three months after the outbreak of the Second World War.

In February 1942, as Flight Lieutenant Terry, 42 Squadron, he was awarded the DFC (Distinguished Flying Cross) for having carried out 41 sorties against enemy shipping off the west coast of German-occupied Norway, and an attack against an enemy airfield at Sola, 10km (6 miles) southwest of Stavanger. Also, in November 1941, he had attacked and hit a merchant ship escorted by two vessels and then flown back safely to base although damage had rendered his wireless unserviceable. The citation said that he had 'always displayed courage, skill and determination'.

During 1943, Kenneth, now promoted to the rank of Squadron Leader, 547 Squadron, was leading anti-submarine and anti-shipping patrols of three aircraft over the Bay of Biscay. He was with Coastal Command at Davidstow airbase in Cornwall, flying patrols which could last up to seven hours.

German U-boats were based in ports in France and in 1943 suffered serious losses, being forced to abandon their bases in the Bay of Biscay in autumn 1944.

Kenneth was killed in action on 26 April 1944 during a flight over Cardigan Bay. He was on a night exercise testing new radar equipment which would greatly assist in detecting the quarry in the dark. The reason for the aircraft's plunge into the sea was never established. All the crew were killed.

Kenneth was a modest man; he enjoyed reading (mainly novels) and listening to classical music. Members of his crew stressed what a brilliant pilot he was. He had always been fascinated by aircraft and flying had been his chosen career. His sister recently wrote: *At the age of 23, he was a Squadron Leader with a DFC. His death was a tragic finale to a life with so much promise.*

Kenneth was buried in Dringhouses Cemetery, where his parents were laid to rest alongside him in 1980 and his brother Richard in 1984.

Kenneth's grave in Dringhouses Cemetery.
(M J Ramsbottom)

A Long Journey Home

John Cranston, the younger brother of Gordon who was killed on 27/28 April 1944, was born in Newcastle in early 1923. His mother was from Dringhouses and the family returned here before the Second World War. Like his brother, John worked for the firm of Cooke, Troughton and Simms. He was allowed to leave in order to join the forces and trained first in Rhodesia, in Induna and Heany (where he got his wings), and then in South Africa, flying over the Indian Ocean during his training with Coastal Command. He returned to the UK and, there being few vacancies for pilots in Coastal Command, he joined 207 Squadron, Bomber Command, based at Spilsby, near Skegness, Lincolnshire, flying Lancasters.

John flew 22 successful missions, including the bombing of targets in Munich, Essen and Hamburg. The 23rd operation, on 14 March 1945, was to bomb the Wintershall synthetic oil plant near Leipzig, but on the way there, in the vicinity of Leipzig, his Lancaster was intercepted by German night-raiders. After a battle, John (as pilot) gave the order for the crew to bale out of his badly-damaged aircraft: there was a big hole in the floor where the radar dome (which gave a picture of the ground) had been blown off and the port engine was on fire. John's aircraft was one of two Lancasters lost on this operation. Such raids were immensely important, carried out as they were deep into Germany whilst the Allied forces were moving slowly east, towards and then across the Rhine. Of this period, Winston Churchill wrote in Volume Six of his account of the Second World War: 'Continuing raids by our heavy bombers had reduced the German oil output to a critical point, ruined many of their airfields, and so heavily damaged their factories and transportation system as to bring them almost to a standstill.'

Two of the crew were unable to get out of the aircraft and were killed when it crashed in a huge explosion (the bombs were still on board). John and the four other crew parachuted to the ground, separated by some distance from each other. John had floated down for only a short time and was later told by another of his crew that the force of the explosion had blown him away from the crash site. He started walking by himself silently eastwards, towards friendly Russian forces, but was picked up by the Germans after a few days. He was taken firstly to an interrogation centre at an aerodrome where he met up briefly with Terry Hannaby, his navigator, and where they noticed some small aeroplanes without propellers. This information concerning the possession by Germany of jet planes was to be of great interest later on.

John was then taken to Halle gaol, north-west of Leipzig, and thence to Dulagluft near Frankfurt for further questioning. Here he made friends with an American

John in his flying days.
(J Cranston collection)

97

private called Tom, and they stuck together; they were both in a large group of 100 prisoners of war being marched by their captors southwards in the direction of Munich when they made an overnight stop in a wooden barn. Tom noticed that the walls were not exactly escape-proof and he and John managed to scrape away the soil at the base of the side of the building and then crawl under and creep away undetected into the night. After two days' walking back the way they had come whilst on the march, they heard shells coming over. Tom realized that it was his compatriots and that they would shoot on sight anything that moved, so he and John moved into the fields alongside the road. When the American tanks stopped nearby, Tom called out and quickly revealed his and John's identity. They were invited to climb into one of the tanks and were offered a drink: a full bottle of Crème de Menthe!! Their hosts turned out to be part of General George Patton's 4th Armoured Division, then sweeping eastwards across Southern Germany, and they arranged for Tom and John to have a lift on a lorry to Paris, which had been liberated on 25 August 1944. For one of the overnight stops during this part of the journey, a very large property was taken over and in the cellar were huge quantities of cherries…

Once in Paris, Tom joined up with the American forces and John with the British and they lost touch with each other for ever. At first, John tried in vain to get back to the UK: in spite of his escape story, he was deemed to be of too lowly a rank to be taken home. However, by chance he met up with the pilot of a twin-engined Avro Anson responsible for the Paris-Croydon shuttle service, who offered John a lift – provided he could be at the aerodrome for 6 am the next day. John was there by 5 am! At Croydon airfield he was asked if he had anything to declare… His arrival had been expected and there was a RAF car waiting to take him to London, where he was interrogated: his sighting of the German jet planes caused much interest. He was told to report back to his squadron; having said it was 'near York', he was given a rail pass to there. Before he set off from London, he sent a telegram to his mother (in North Lane), who several weeks before had been told that he was missing, to give her the news. He then caught a train north to get back home to Dringhouses. He visited his friends at Cooke, Troughton and Simms' works, and after two weeks' holiday (which he felt he deserved) he rejoined his squadron at Spilsby. Much to his surprise, no-one was expecting him!

Between baling out of his Lancaster near Leipzig and arriving back in York, John had covered about 1600 km (1000 miles). The war in Europe ended on 8 May, but even if it had been prolonged, John, being an 'escaper', would not have carried out any further operations. His war service finished in July 1945, when he was still only 22 years old. An amazing story, one might say. John thinks otherwise: *No, not at all. You act through instinct, to evade capture.* Nevertheless, such exploits deserve to be remembered.

John's Caterpillar Club badge (actual length 1.9cm (0.75")). Anyone whose life is saved by a parachute becomes a member of the Caterpillar Club, so called because parachutes are made of silk spun by silkworms (caterpillars). (M E Lord)

Remembering Courage and Sacrifice

Reminders of the two World Wars include photographs and other memorabilia treasured by families, film archives, dedicated museums, war graves and former airfields and wartime structures. One reminder now rarely encountered is the evocative sound of the Lancaster bomber, which many of us remember from our childhood or youth and recognize instantly. However, the most widespread are our war memorials. Found at the heart of our communities, they serve as permanent reminders of the sacrifices made and dangers overcome during the two global conflicts of the 20th century.

Remembrance Day, 8 November 2009, Dringhouses War Memorial. (R T Smith)